Lights Out!

The Memoir of
Nursing Sister Kate Wilson
Canadian Army Medical Corps
1915-1917

By

Kate M. Wilson

Katharine Wilson-Simmie

CEF BOOKS
2004

National Library of Canada Cataloguing In Publication

Wilson-Simmie, Katherine M.

Lights Out : The Memoir of Nursing Sister Katherine Wilson, Canadian Army Medical Corps,1915-1917 / by Katherine Wilson Simmie.

First ed. published: Belleview, Ont. : Mika, 1981.
ISBN 1-896979-27-0

1. Wilson-Simmie, Katherine M. 2. World War, 1914-1918--Medical care--Canada. 3. World War, 1914-1918--Personal narratives, Canadian. 4. Canada. Canadian Army. Royal Canadian Army Medical Corps--Biography. 5. Nurses--Canada--Biography. I. Title

D630.W5A3 2003   940.4'7571'092   C2003-900640-9

Published by: **CEF BOOKS**
                P.O. Box 40083
                Ottawa, Ontario
                K1V 0W8, Canada
                613-823-7000
                cefbooks@rogers.com

Previously published by Mikra Publishing, 1981, 0-919303-51-X.

Acknowledgments: The publisher would like to thank Helen Simmie Godden for her cooperation in the production of this book. The contribution of Clayton Robichaud and Lachlan Christie is also recognized.

Front cover: Fifty Canadian Nursing Sisters en route to France, June 1915.
Back cover: Nursing Sister Kate Wilson, 1915.

Preface to the 2004 Edition

Lights Out! is a unique memoir chronicling the service of a Canadian Army Medical Corps Nursing Sister in the Great War. It is the charming story of Kate Wilson, a farm girl from rural Ontario, who enlists at Ottawa in 1915 and serves in hospitals in England, France, and with the CAMC in the Aegean.

The historical value of *Lights Out!* makes the decision to resurrect it an easy one. It is one of only two Canadian Nursing Sister memoirs that I know of. (The other, *Our Bit* by Mabel Clint was published in 1934.) It covers, in beautiful detail, a forgotten episode of the war; the story of the Canadian hospitals sent to the island of Lemnos, in the Aegean. They were to provide additional medical services in support of the last major offensive of the Gallipoli Campaign in August 1915.

However historically significant Kate Wilson's memoir is, it is the exceptional character of the author that shines through and brings this story to life. Mrs. Wilson-Simmie (she married Captain Robert Simmie, MC, in 1917) was a woman of great determination, strength, and charm, with a brilliant sense of humour. In many ways she was a wide-eyed tourist exploring exotic places like London, Paris, Cairo and the Pyramids. Kate saw places she never dreamed she would. But beyond the sight-seeing was the deadly backdrop of war. Her postings included several front-line hospitals and a Casualty Clearing Station a few miles from the fighting. She handled her responsibilities with great courage and a sense of devotion so typical of Nursing Sisters to the wounded "boys".

Due to the kindness of her eldest daughter, Helen Godden, this book contains many original photographs from Kate's personal album.

I have myself travelled Miss Wilson's route. I have been to Portianos. The church visited by Sister Wilson and Padre Frost is still there and beside it is Portianos Military Cemetery. The graves of Matron Jaggard and Sister Munro rest amongst 350 other Commonwealth graves. Visiting them is a lonely experience. The point where the Canadian hospitals were located is now barren, with the exception of a Moslem cemetery containing the graves of many Egyptian labourers and Turkish prisoners. Mudros harbour is very quiet now, virtually empty. Myrina, known as Kastro in 1915, is still the main village on the island, and its old Byzantine fort is still a magnificent ruin and a very hot climb. The sunsets are simply magnificent

In France, all that remains of the major Etaples Depot is the massive cemetery containing 11,000 burials, including many Nurses. Of course Paris-Plage and Le Treport are still resorts, but for another generation. Boulogne and Calais remain busy ports, but now for the cross-channel tourists. The coastal cliffs near the towns are lined with massive bunkers, reminders of the Second World War. Not far away is Calais Canadian War Cemetery, containing 594 Canadian graves. These are the graves of Canadian men who died liberating the Channel ports in 1944. Near Wimereux, where John McCrae is buried, you can still see Napoleon's massive column, and Miss Wilson's "happy valley" at Terlincthun. It now contains a Commonwealth cemetery, containing the graves of 4,400 First World War soldiers who died in nearby Allied hospitals.

The same is true of Puchevillers, the site of No. 44 Casualty Clearing Station. All that remains is a Commonwealth War Graves Cemetery, containing 1,839 graves, mostly of soldiers who died at No. 44. Amongst them is the grave of Private Gordon, and in the German plot of 74 graves rests the young German soldier who died so courageously on Sister Wilson's watch.

Through her thoughtful memoir Kate Wilson-Simmie takes us back in time and brings all these people and places to life.

To help understand the historical context of the memoir I have added a few notes on the Nursing Sisters of the Canadian Army Medical Corps regarding their duties, theatres of operation and the dangers of service.

Background - War 1914-1915

At the outbreak of war in August 1914, Canada, with a population of 8 million, had a permanent military force of 3,500 men. Included in this meagre force were cavalry, infantry, artillery, engineers and a small medical establishment that included five permanent force Nursing Sisters. Nationally there was a sizeable, if poorly trained, militia from which Canada would draw a volunteer force of 30,000 men. At

Valcartier, Quebec, in August and September 1914 the volunteers were drawn together in units, lightly trained and ,in October 1914, shipped to England. Known as the First Contingent, Canada's initial contribution to the war included many Canadian Army Medical Corps units including three Field Ambulances, two General Hospitals, two Stationary Hospitals and 101 Nursing Sisters. On reaching England the First Contingent found a somewhat confused reception. None-the-less the British had a real need for all available medical resources and in November 1914 the first Canadians went to France. The honour to be "First" fell to No. 2 Canadian Stationary Hospital, which arrived at Le Touquet on November 8th.

It was clear that Canada would need more Nurses and a draft was sent over in early 1915. Amongst their number was a 5'6", 28 year-old trained nurse from Chatsworth, Ontario, Katharine Mildred Wilson.

In the winter of 1915 another Canadian hospital was moved to France and with it came the call for more Sisters. The Canadian women were utilized in a number of locales where they would get training and experience. The war had taken a ruthless turn in April 1915 when the Germans released chlorine gas on unsuspecting French and Canadian troops. The Huns had indicated there were to be no more rules of war, from now on all targets were fair game. This meant none were safe and as the war progressed Hospital ships became the prey for German U-boats.

April 1915 also opened a new theatre of war in Turkey. On April 25th, 1915, British, Australian and New Zealand troops landed on a small peninsula on the European side of the Dardanelles. The Gallipoli Campaign was officially underway.

Gallipoli, 1915

The objective of the Gallipoli campaign was to capture the Dardanelles, advance to Istanbul and knock the Turks, who were allied with the Germans, out of the war. The landing on April 25th, 1915 succeeded in obtaining a foothold on the peninsula, but failed to win a convincing victory. Over the next two months French, British, Australian, Indian and New Zealander troops tried to deliver a knockout blow to their Turkish foes but the attacks failed due to stiff opposition and inadequate munitions.

After a period of stalemate the Allies decided on a major offensive in August 1915. Before the attack could be launched new divisions had to be in place, with the supplies and infrastructure to support them. This included adequate medical facilities. Throughout the Gallipoli campaign treatment of the wounded had been woefully inadequate, and this often meant the wounded had to be transported to Malta or Egypt, and sometimes directly to England. The conditions on the ships were often horribly unsanitary and many died before making it to a hospital.

For the upcoming offensive the British planned to expand the facilities on the Greek island of Lemnos (Limnos), 100 km southwest of Gallipoli, which had acted as a depot since April 1915. They were provided with two units: the No.1 and No.3 Canadian Stationary Hospitals. Amongst the staff of the No. 3 CSH was Nursing Sister Kate Wilson.

Canadian Hospitals go to the Mediterranean

The journey to Lemnos seemed to be a pleasure cruise to the Canadians, but in fact it was anything but. In 1915 German U-boats had infiltrated the Mediterranean, and this new technology wreaked havoc on Allied shipping, including transports ships and hospital ships. In August 1915 The Germans sank the troopship *Royal Edward* with the loss of 900 lives and in October the *Marquette* went down and 167 lives were lost, including 10 New Zealander Nursing Sisters. In 1915 alone German U-boats accounted for 92 vessels. The Mediterranean was as dangerous as any battlefield in 1915. In November 1916, the *Britannic,* the sister ship of the *Titanic* was sunk in the Mediterranean. (It is remarkable how many of the ships that Kate Wilson encountered -the *Asturias, Salta*, *Hesperian*, *Royal Edward*, *Britannic* were sunk.)

After a brief stay in Egypt, the two units arrived in Lemnos and set up their camps under the most deplorable conditions. But within a few days theywere receiving sick and wounded soldiers from Gallipoli. By the Fall of 1915 the campaign was winding down and battle casualties were replaced by those suffering from dysentery. The circumstances were terrible for all and dysentery claimed the lives of a Canadian Matron and a Nursing Sister of No.3 CSH. It was remarkable more did not succumb. In December 1915 the British and Anzacs evacuated their positions at Suvla Bay and Anzac Cove. In January 1916 the troops were withdrawn from the final Allied position on Cape Helles and the Gallipoli campaign was over. It had been a dismal failure.

The Canadian hospital units were taken to Alexandria, Egypt in February 1916, where they remained until they were either transferred back to France, or sent to support a new campaign in northern Greece at Salonica (Thessaloniki). Amongst those fortunate enough to be returned to Europe was Sister Wilson. (one of those who ended up in Salonica was a Canadian Army Medical Corps orderly by the name of Lester Pearson, later to become Prime Minister of Canada.)

The French Coast

Once the Canadian hospitals returned from the Mediterranean they were quickly moved to positions on the Channel coast. The French coast between Calais and Le Treport was a continuous military facility, with all varieties of hospitals, troop and training depots (Etaples was home to the infamous Bull Ring), and all forms of munition and supplies. It was the hub of the British military effort in France. Even more importantly in the spring of 1916 the British Army was not only expanding their frontlines, but preparing for their greatest offensive of the war. To accommodate the wounded of their anticipated attack medical support was being expanded.

When Sister Wilson returned to France in April 1916, she was surprised at how much the hospital facilities had changed. They had taken on a far more elaborate state of organization since 1915 and a far more permanent appearance.

When the British Army launched its great "Push" on July 1st, 1916, their hopes for an easy victory were quickly dashed when they lost 60,000 men on its first day. Such losses put a tremendous strain on the base hospitals, and closer to the fighting on the Casualty Clearing Stations. The CCS was the closest to the front where surgery was done. It was at the CCS where the most severely wounded were treated, and the decision was made who was likely to live and who was likely to die.

In early July Sister Wilson was assigned to No. 44 Imperial (British) CCS at Puchevillers, 15 km northwest of Albert. It was at No .44 she encountered the most distressing cases of her nursing service. In her 48 bed ward only a handful would survive a 24 hour period. She cared for the dying with great compassion and was deeply affected by her experience. She remained at No. 44 until the end of the Somme Offensive in November 1916. Its cost to the British Empire was 250,000 casualties, including 24,000 Canadians.

After four months at No. 44 CCS Kate Wilson was transferred back to the CAMC. Shortly after she fell ill and never totally recovered. In January 1917 she returned to Canada and in March resigned her position with the Overseas Military Forces of Canada. Kate Wilson's war was over.

The Canadian Nursing Service

During the Great War 2,504 Canadian Nursing Sisters served overseas. In total 39 Sisters died. Twenty-one died in action and 18 died of disease . The worst loss was when 14 Canadian Sisters drowned when the Hospital Ship Llandovery Castle was sunk by a German U-boat in June 1918. Another Sister was lost when the Leinster was sunk in October 1918. Six other Nursing Sisters were killed in German bombing raids on hospitals at Etaples and Doullens in May 1918. Statistically, Canadian Nursing Sisters paid a very high price as non-combatants in the First World War.

The Nursing Sisters won 378 Decorations, including 321 Awards of the Royal Red Cross, and 8 Military Medals for Bravery in the Field. In addition 169 Sisters were Mentioned in Despatches. Theirs was a very noble war.

Kate Wilson was one of 600,000 Canadians who served in the Great War. She belonged to a generation which honoured Canada, served with great courage and pride, and left a legacy that should never be forgotten. *Lights Out!* is one woman's contribution to keeping her generation's legacy alive.

Norm Christie
Ottawa,

September 2004.

To those of the Third Unit of the

Canadian Army Medical Corps

who worked together in World War I

in France and at the Dardanelles,

and who formed a deep, sincere

bond of respect and affection.

Foreword

I have often wondered why no book has been written by a Canadian Army Nursing Sister, of her experiences on active duty during the First or Second World War. There were so many interesting stories that might have been told about this element of Canada's involvement.

Following my discharge from the army after the First War, I used my diary to write such a book, not for publication, but rather as a souvenir for my children, while the facts were still fresh in my memory. I have read many books written by men, and though these were well written, many tended to romanticize events. Alan Moorehead's "Gallipoli" gave the most authentic account of the Dardanelles campaign. And Lester Pearson's *"Mike; Volume I"* contributed valuable information. Well, I have been there too.

I have had many puzzling points clarified, as I read these old war stories. How the Blockade was accomplished; the origin of the tank. When tanks first went into operation on the Somme front I was on duty there in No.3 Imperial hospital. Now, since I have, for some time, been retired, and more or less an arthritic cripple, I have a tremendous desire to tell my story, in my own way, and to try to provide a clear picture of the life of a Canadian Army Nursing Sister during the 1914-1918 World War. I tell of the Dardanelles, of the people, the country, and our pioneer service; of a palace in France; of duty in canvas tents; a long holiday in Egypt, the pyramids and Cairo.

I trust you may enjoy reading my account, as I have enjoyed writing it.

Table of Contents

Chapter One

War

I do not remember exactly what we were talking about, though I'm sure we discussed over sweet, warm tea and biscuits, how I was to be safely transported from Manitoba back to my home in Owen Sound, Ontario. I was visiting an old friend, an English doctor, who had come with his wife to practise medicine in Canada, and we had resolved that the train was by far the best method of transport when the door flew open and a woman, whom I later learned to be the doctor's neighbour, burst excitedly into the room, loudly announcing that war had been declared in Belgium.

I found her behaviour quite startling and herself quite rude, breaking in upon us in that manner, but what was more striking was her attitude. There seemed to be a great thrill in her voice, as if she found it the best of news that Belgium was involved in a war. Yet I found it difficult to understand, in that instant, how the difficulties of a small country separated from Canada by some two thousand miles of salt water could be the cause of such excitement in a woman living in Manitoba. Certainly it did not excite me at the time. But her enthusiasm was like a push broom sweeping over our sudden silence.

"Several men of the militia have already been placed on guard at the bridge!" she went on, clasping her hands together. There was a short break for a moment, and her face glowed with wonder.

"Oh! Do you think our boys will have to go to war?" she asked with the greatest of concern. She seemed to think how thrilling that would be; boys wearing uniforms, trooping off to war, all swelled with drama and self-pride.

Her stay was as short as it was sudden, for with a last ecstatic handclasp and a shrill "oooh" she was off to spread news of war throughout the town. I'm sure everyone heard of the war that day.

When she had gone I turned to the Doctor. "But why on earth have they placed guards at a local bridge here because of some war in Belgium?" I asked.

The Doctor was an old military man, and had taken the news with an unexpected gravity. Perhaps he had a greater understanding of world affairs than I, but his mood and tone took on such a serious aspect that I began to feel it would be best if I left as soon as possible. If it did prove to be a real war, I thought, and if Canadian men went to fight, then Canadian nurses would have to follow to tend the injured.

We finished our tea, though our previous discussion of train journeys had lost its importance.

When I did eventually arrive back in Owen Sound I was surprised to find that two of my former classmates had already enlisted. They treated the whole affair more or less as a joke, or at least they seemed to, as they drilled in the streets, still wearing their civilian dress and smiling with cocky assurance at the girls who lined the walks to watch them. I stood on a street corner with Doctor T.H. Middlebro watching them pass by, their boots drumming heavily on the road. The doctor watched them in silence, his face unmoving. Then, with his pensive eyes upon them he murmured, "Fodder for cannon," a chilling analogy that brought sudden and horrible pictures to my mind.

I was later to remember his remark and the sadness in his eyes, magnified by the thick spectacles he wore. And I would later compare the horrors I had pictured in my mind with the painful realities I was to see, hear and smell.

My imagination could not hope to compete with the anguish of reality.

Yet at that time I, myself, was restless and uncertain. Several members of the Board of Education had vetoed my decision to serve for my country. I could not tell for certain if this was due to a lack of patriotism on their part, or if they simply believed that it was improper for a woman to subject herself to the indignities of war. Yet I was adamant in my desire to go. As the days passed, the situation in Europe grew more threatening. Our boys were donning Khaki. Everyone was bursting with pride in our nation, and I was as affected by this patriotic fervour as anyone else.

I would go because I wanted to go. Yet how was I to get there?

Then one day a telegram arrived for me from a cousin in Ottawa, who was on the staff of Sir Sam Hughes, then the Minister of Defense.

It read: "CONTINGENT OF NURSES BEING COMPILED STOP DO YOU WISH TO GO?"

Did I wish to go! Nothing on earth could have stopped me once I was on my way to the telegraph office with my reply. Shortly, the second message arrived.

"Hold yourself in readiness for further orders."

My head swam with the words, "I'm going, I'm going." A whirling in my mind bespoke my intense excitement.

My fiance, Duncan, had recently died of typhoid fever. I felt that had Duncan lived he would have been as enthusiastic as I and would have been one of the first to offer himself. Now I was offering myself in his place. My chance had come unexpectedly. Until the moment when the first telegram had arrived from Ottawa, every approach I'd made to any member of the Board of Education, regarding my enlisting, had met with refusal. Then too, my own conscience bothered me. I had accepted School Medical Inspection work voluntarily. How could I leave when I had signed a contract? But the wire from Ottawa was my answer.

Tossing conscience aside, and with a firm step, I walked from the telegraph office to the office of the Chairman of the School Board.

"Mr. Smith," I said, "I am enlisting." I handed him the telegram. "I have answered that telegram and I intend to go."

Mr. Smith sat back in his chair, holding the telegram and furrowing his brow. A very displeased expression drew over his face.

"You cannot simply walk off a job like that. Not when you've signed a contract specifying a definite period of service. Forget this nonsense of enlisting. You're needed here just as badly." He pushed the telegram away with impatience.

"I'm sorry Mr. Smith, but I've approached you before concerning this. I shall not be dissuaded now. Not with this." I picked up the telegram and held it before him. Then I reached into my bag and drew out an envelope I had had with me on every visit to the School Board since I'd decided to enlist.

"Here is my official resignation in letter form." I dropped it before him on his desk. He stared at me as if I were completely mad. I stared back at him.

"I'm leaving and that is final," I said and, turning on my heel, I left his office. If Mr. Smith thought that I was absolutely mad, then I, in turn, thought that he was the most unpatriotic Canadian I had ever met.

There followed the days when I waited for the orders that would send me to God knew where. They were anxious times, and I was tense with the waiting. Finally I was ordered to board a train for Ottawa. Well, I had been positive in my desire to go to war. I had fought and argued with people who had been my co-workers and friends and I had won my own victory.

But this did not prevent me from feeling pangs of homesickness as the train pulled from the station and rounded the curve, blocking my home from my sight.

Ottawa

I got off the train in Ottawa to find the station almost overflowing with women. Some stood in groups, some alone, others wandered to and fro. Many seemed lost, asking porters for directions. Others moved positively with definite purpose in their stride. There were tall women and short, stout and lean, some delicate and elegant in their mannerisms. I had never seen so many women gathered in one spot before, and I remember peering intently at several and wondering if any one of them in particular would become my friend. At home and school I had always had a friend. But there was no way of telling then. We were all so busy trying to get settled, some heading off towards the hotels and others, such as myself, simply waiting to be met by friends. As I stood waiting with my bags at my feet I was thrilled with a sense of adventure, and then I wondered if it was just an adventure and not something more!

The following day we were met by the Senior Army Nurse. She was friendly enough in a very official way. She answered questions and told us how to go about securing our gear. We were responsible for fitting ourselves, it seemed. After this brief period of instruction came several busy days of shopping and getting our equipment together. Kid gloves, travelling gear, army boots, were all issued because everything had to be strictly official. As it turned out, it was almost worth your life to have the white piping on the collar of your navy blue jacket wider that the prescribed sixteenth of an inch, or your blue felt army hat tilted at an angle, rather than absolutely vertical.

Kate Wilson at 15 Rosedale Avenue, Ottawa, 1915.

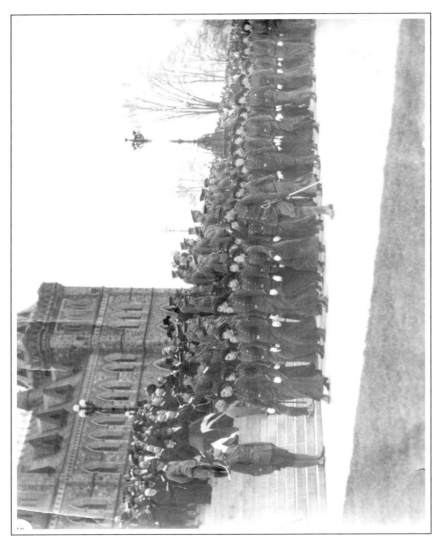

Our first parade as a unit and last picture taken the day we left for overseas service.

Yet despite the seemingly haphazard system of outfitting, the day finally came when we were all assembled and equipped. Our uniforms were a light, sky blue cotton with twin rows of brass military buttons down the front. The epaulettes on the shoulders were fitted with two First Lieutenant's stars, indicating our rank in the Army Medical Corps. Under the epaulettes ran the straps of the fitted white aprons. These crossed at the back and were fastened to the apron belts, and over the waist belt we wore our firm Sam Brown leather belts fastened in front by two lion's head brass buckles. I never did know the origin of the lions' heads on the Sam Brown belt, but our medical brass buttons bore the sign of the rod and snake. In the story of the children of Israel, in the book of Exodus, the rod and snake was the sign of healing, a sign drawn from the rod, given to Moses by God, which devoured the two snakes in the Pharaoh's court.

With our uniforms for day service we wore sheer white veils, as introduced by Florence Nightingale in the Crimean War. These were folded and worn over our heads so the back hung gracefully over the shoulders. Oh, we loved it all. Our dress uniform was made of navy blue serge and was exactly the same as our day service uniforms with the exception of the starched white cuffs and collars. The navy jacket was fitted with a high, round collar of the same blue serge material and edged with two narrow scarlet and white bands. The cuffs of the sleeves were also edged with scarlet. The Sam Brown belt was omitted and replaced with one of blue serge and two lion's head buckles. With this uniform we could either wear our navy hats or our white veil. Either was proper. There was a heavy, long, navy blue military coat and also a navy blue cape lined with scarlet to be worn over either uniform if the weather was bad. With a pair of high black boots and a pair of black lisle stockings our Canadian Army Medical Corps uniform was complete.

I was staying with my Aunt in Ottawa, and I remember looking at all my kit lying on her large bed. I was thrilled and yet at the same moment had a slight shiver of trepidation. After gathering all that gear it had come time for our first inspection. Oh, I was certainly excited at the thought of wearing my new uniform (for if it made the man it certainly made the woman!), but I was more than a bit concerned at the thought of attiring myself to perfection and then facing the mile-long walk I had to make from my Aunt's home to the Department of Militia. But then, if I intended to be a soldier, I had better start being one. With every buckle in place and an extra dab of powder on my nose (to prove to myself that even in my excitement I was still in a normal state of mind) I found myself prepared to meet the inspection. With a last quick survey in the mirror and a final salute to the slight, uniformed reflection staring back at me, I set out, head up, eyes front, and heart pounding.

As I walked I felt somewhat self-conscious. Perhaps it was the effect of wearing a military uniform. But what I remember feeling most was concern over what I should do if I met a Canadian officer (even a sergeant ... yes, even a private!) on my journey. Salute? Well perhaps. Smile? Well hardly. Yet it had to be faced and so I strode on, not feeling nearly so soldierly as my mirrored image had appeared, for down inside myself I was still a very shy, country girl.

"Leaving tonight." Never ever again do I expect to get such a thrill out of two small words.

The day had been a busy one for we new "Canadian Army Nursing Sisters" - such a long title, especially when you added on the appendage "of the British Expeditionary Force". After the Senior Canadian Army Nursing Sister had made her last inspection we paraded en masse to the Parliament Buildings for a review by the Governor General, the Duke of Connaught, and by Sir Sam Hughes, the Minister of Defence. After that we marched to the Chateau Laurier to pose for pictures.

Did I say marched? To a trained soldier we must have looked more than a little ridiculous. Indeed, it was our first attempt at walking in unison, never so easy a feat as it appears. We must have presented a pathetic picture as we strode along. But we kept our heads up and we certainly did try to look military.

That night we all queued at the station, waiting to board the train. Many had friends from home to bid them "bon voyage" and "fare thee well." I had bid my aunt "adieu" at her home and so had no one at the station to see me off. I was just beginning to feel far from home already when I spied a tall figure frantically waving both arms in the air to attract my attention. It was a very undignified display from the sedate Doctor H.G. Collins, Head of the Geographical Survey of Canada, but

Nursing Sister Kate Wilson, 1915.

Canadian Nursing Sisters the day before leaving overseas; Chateau Laurier. Kate Wilson; front row, far left. 68 Nurses in total.

I loved him for it. In his buoyant and frantic farewell, his eager arms waving above the swarm of heads, I saw all that was dear to me, home and friends, as if extending a last good-bye, as I headed out into a new and strange life.

It doesn't seem enough to blow a kiss and wave goodbye to all that you know, not knowing what it is you are facing. But when you must enter that unknown you brush away your tears; and when they call your name during the roll call, you answer, keeping all that stirs within you, inside.

For the most part the trip to Halifax was uneventful. There was the constant motion of the train, the skimming of the countryside and sound of the train going on and on like some untiring beast of burden. At the stops there were sometimes bands that played for us, cheerful in the mornings as they played "Colonel Bogey's March", or solemn with "Land of Hope and Glory", as if weighing on us an unspoken promise. But the promise was there, we knew it. Sometimes we thought of it in quiet moments though I do not think that we spoke of it that much, except between friends.

On our arrival at Halifax we were disappointed to find that there were orders for us to stay in our coaches - our first war orders. I'm sure some of us had forgotten in a way, that we were in the army and that orders were orders. But after a time we were transferred to the troop ship *Hesperian* which plied regularly between Halifax and Liverpool.

Her sides were bleak grey, with black streaks of rippling waves painted against her sides to make her as inconspicuous as possible to enemy ships.

Inside, the round port-holes were draped with black cloth that was drawn at night, covering the whole window so our lights would not be visible. The distance at which even a small light can be seen while at sea during the blackness of the night is incredible.

The rules were very strict and rigidly enforced while on board ship: no lighting of matches or smoking cigarettes on deck, no whistles were to be blown, and white handkerchiefs were forbidden. At all times we had to wear a Red Cross on our uniforms, even though we were Army nurses and not members of the Red Cross. These, incidentally, were discarded as soon as we reached Liverpool. Only during the daytime were we allowed to walk up and down the open decks. At night we had to remain in our cabins or in the lounge area, where we played bridge or danced or held a sing-song. Often at night we could hear the soft padding of many feet and the muted voices of the officers. Shrouded in darkness and silence, masked with paint and low to the water, the ship was made as inconspicuous as possible in every way.

Yet despite all these precautions, the *Hesperian* was torpedoed some months later by a German submarine. Captain Beattie survived the sinking and was transferred to a troop ship on the Mediterranean. In 1915 he visited our hospital, unit No. 3, Canadian Stationary Hospital, while we were on duty at the Dardanelles.

During our first night on board ship we sat quietly, a subdued group of women. There was a definite anti-climactic atmosphere. Thus far, fear had never really entered my mind, and that first night it was difficult to understand whether or not I did feel afraid. In any case, I was dreadfully practical about my situation, writing a Last-Will-and-Testament sort of letter to my sister, grinning as I dropped it in the mail bag that would be collected before we sailed. I wondered in what vein she would interpret it. Some hours later, we heard the sound of the engines and we knew that we were on our way.

It was hot and stuffy in my stateroom, with its three bunks, and I felt very uncomfortable. And so it was that I turned to my two companions saying, "I think I'll have a bath."

"Billy," piped up Peggy Smith, "I think that you'd better stay dirty for one night. You'll live through it."

I thought she was being quite ridiculous. Even if I lived through it I would certainly be most uncomfortable.

"Well," said Peg, "have you ever taken a bath on board a ship while she's in motion?"

"No, I've never taken a bath on a stuffy old ship before," I said.

Well, don't say we didn't warn you," said Sister Cook from her position on the bunk, looking up bemusedly from her book. I was never one to back out of something I had set my mind to. Perhaps that best explains why I was on board a troopship in the first place. So I armed myself with soap and a towel and proceeded to the bathroom. But for some unknown reason, my feet did not seem to react properly. They stepped where they shouldn't have stepped, and the ceiling seemed unnaturally low, even for a ship, and the air was remarkably stuffy.

UNIT *C. A. M. C.*   Regimental No.

ATTESTATION PAPER.

CANADIAN OVER-SEAS EXPEDITIONARY FORCE.

QUESTIONS TO BE PUT BEFORE ATTESTATION.

(ANSWERS).

1. What is your name ? *Katharine Mildred Wilson (Kate)*
2. In what Town, Township or Parish, and in what Country were you born ? *Chatsworth, Ontario, Canada*
3. What is the name of your next-of-kin ? *Susan Wilson*
4. What is the address of your next-of-kin ? *Chatsworth, Ontario, Canada*
5. What is the date of your birth ? *October 15th 1887*
6. What is your Trade or Calling ? *Professional Nurse*
7. Are you married ? *No*
8. Are you willing to be vaccinated or re-vaccinated ? *Yes*
9. Do you now belong to the Active Militia ? *Yes*
10. Have you ever served in any Military Force ? *No*
    If so, state particulars of former Service.
11. Do you understand the nature and terms of your engagement ? *Yes*
12. Are you willing to be attested to serve in the CANADIAN OVER-SEAS EXPEDITIONARY FORCE ? *Yes*

Katharine M. Wilson (Signature of Man).

Alma O. Dawley (Signature of Witness).

DECLARATION TO BE MADE BY MAN ON ATTESTATION.

I, *Katharine Mildred Wilson*, do solemnly declare that the above answers made by me to the above questions are true, and that I am willing to fulfil the engagements by me now made, and I hereby engage and agree to serve in the **Canadian Over-Seas Expeditionary Force**, and to be attached to any arm of the service therein, for the term of one year, or during the war now existing between Great Britain and Germany should that war last longer than one year, and for six months after the termination of that war provided His Majesty should so long require my services, or until legally discharged.

Date *May 12th* 1915.   *Katharine M. Wilson* (Signature of Recruit).

Alma O. Dawley (Signature of Witness).

OATH TO BE TAKEN BY MAN ON ATTESTATION.

I, *Katharine Mildred Wilson* do make Oath, that I will be faithful and bear true Allegiance to His Majesty **King George the Fifth**, His Heirs and Successors, and that I will as in duty bound honestly and faithfully defend His Majesty, His Heirs and Successors, in Person, Crown and Dignity, against all enemies, and will observe and obey all orders of His Majesty, His Heirs and Successors, and of all the Generals and Officers set over me. So help me God.

Katharine M. Wilson (Signature of Recruit).

Date *May 12th* 1915.   *Alma O. Dawley* (Signature of Witness).

CERTIFICATE OF MAGISTRATE.

The Recruit above-named was cautioned by me that if he made any false answer to any of the above questions he would be liable to be punished as provided in the Army Act.

The above questions were then read to the Recruit in my presence.

I have taken care that he understands each question, and that his answer to each question has been duly entered as replied to, and the said Recruit has made and signed the declaration and taken the oath before me, at *London, England* this *12th* day of *May* 1915.

J. Todd (Signature of Justice).

I certify that the above is a true copy of the Attestation of the above-named Recruit.

J. Todd (Approving Officer).

Maj. C.A.M.C.

L.13506 31-12-14 5,000.

When I reached the bathroom, I sat on the edge of the tub and watched the green water slowly increase in depth.

A queer feeling possessed me. Picking up courage, I stepped into the vile looking liquid and sat down. When the ship rolled left, so did I. When we slowly rolled in the opposite direction I couldn't help but follow, rolling from side to side with the green water lolling back and forth with soft, wet sounds and little noises that went "lap" under my chin as the water swelled up over my neck. And all this time my tummy, poor old thing, kept perfect rhythm with the ship, whatever contents it might have retained rolling in time with the tub water, until finally I felt that I might as well die there as anywhere else.

Ah, but the heart of the military officer surfaced anew. Surely dying in a pool of green water was an undignified end for a Canadian officer, a First Lieutenant in the Canadian Army Medical Corps. And so I dragged myself out and wended my way weakly to my state-room. Wiser, yes, decidedly wiser. After the first day at sea everything was a joy. That is, after the breakfast table ceased to rise slowly to meet one, calling for a hasty retreat to the washroom. We played shuffleboard and bridge, along with other activities, to make our voyage as pleasant as possible. No, we didn't have the luxuries of the modern liners, but the men did their best to make us comfortable.

There were other activities created for our entertainment. The most enjoyable times for me were the long talks with Father O'Leary, and a very fine gentleman he was. The Sisters of the Roman Catholic faith were very fortunate in having such a devout leader. Colonel Gunn of Calgary, Alberta had his men of the Ambulance Corps. put on an impromptu concert on the second deck. While it was enjoyed by all of us, it had a bit of a melancholy theme, and, we hoped, not appropriate to the occasion, as they sang "Asleep in the Deep" and "At Eventide". We were all moved to tears when they finished with "Our Ain Folk".

From my diary:

"Attended our first church service. Owing to the incompetence of the Padres as sailors the service was conducted by Captain Beattie of the ship, a very large man with a long gray beard (I always had pictured a Sea Captain as having a long beard). After we were all seated, in he strode, looking neither to right or left, opened the ship's bible service book, and without any more ado proceeded as quickly as possible to get through the order of service. With a final "That's all" he stalked out, leaving us sitting, looking at each other. However, to make ourselves feel that we had really been to Church, we held a sing-song of our own. While the *Hesperian* ploughed her way through the gray waters of the Atlantic Ocean, an air of reverence seemed to fall over the group of Nursing Sisters as we rose and sang together:

Eternal father strong to save,
Whose arm has bound the restless wave.
Who bid the mighty ocean deep
It's own appointed limits keep,
Oh, hear us when we cry to thee
For those in peril on the sea.

Never had the words of this dignified old hymn been insignificant for me, yet as I stood and looked out over the rolling waves, it seemed to me that at that very moment, an enemy could be haunting our pathway. It was a comfort to be reminded that we had our Eternal Father, strong and willing to save, and encouragement to put right first in the days that lay ahead of us.

There were exciting stories afloat, of a boat having been sunk sometime during the night, and that the *Hesperian* was being chased by a German submarine. Never have the whistles blown. Travelling as we are in the dark every night, with all port holes covered with black drapes, we begin to feel that we really are nearing the seat of war, as well as nearing our destination. We expect to land around 8 p.m..."

When we came up from dinner, it was to find the waters all around us infested with small boats, as we were approaching Liverpool harbour. In the distance we could see a small boat signalling. This, we learned, was the pilot ship. As we drew nearer a smaller motor boat could be seen coming toward the *Hesperian*. What a thrill, what sighs of relief! As it drew nearer the engines were stopped and a ladder lowered over the side of the ship, for the Officer who was standing, waiting to come aboard. As he climbed the wobbly ladder we all gave him a hearty Canadian cheer of welcome, and partly of gratitude, knowing that we had arrived safely. It was then that we learned that the previous Friday at 2 a.m. the *Lusitania*, an American ship, had been torpedoed by a German submarine. We also learned from our bearded Captain Beattie that our ship had been receiving messages all day to keep off the coast line and away from land, resulting in our going many miles off course. Every sailor was up and dressed the whole night through, while we slept peacefully, never dreaming of the danger so close to all of us. Perhaps we did not sleep so peacefully or were so comfortable, but now we understood why we had been ordered to wear our life-belts day and night, ever since Friday. How we had blessed the pesky things - but army orders must be obeyed. By 9 p.m. we were in the harbour. I think that most of us sent up a prayer of thanksgiving. Everyone was up the following morning by 6 a.m., packed and ready to leave the ship that had begun to feel like home. First the men went down the gang-plank and stood in formation. Then came the Nursing Sisters and Officers. Goodbyes were said with a feeling of misgiving, and we wondered if ever we might meet again. The majority of Officers were connected with the army, and would soon be joining their various regiments. Might we, as nurse and patient, meet some day in some field hospital? One could not tell what might happen in these uncertain days of war.

England

At last we were in England. It was a misty morning, though the sun tried to break through, creating a lovely scene of the harbour packed with ships of every description, from launches to battle destroyers. An odd little train was waiting for us, doing its best to look important, as it sniffed and snorted with an air of impatience. We were all marched on board and packed like sardines into the small, two-seated coaches that boasted white crocheted tidies on the back of each seat.

A shrill whistle, as if someone had given the little train a pinch behind and we were off, travelling through the most beautiful green countryside. What a relief after days of travelling through the gray waters of the Atlantic ocean. At Crewe we stopped to pick up baskets of food; rolls without butter, cookies (English sweets) and coffee. We had our first glimpse of an English castle as we sped quickly along. When we came to a hill, large or small, did we go up and over, puffing and panting, as any good Canadian train would? Oh no! We slipped clean through a tunnel. A moment's darkness and suddenly we were out in bright sunshine once more.

On our arrival at Charing Cross depot Matron MacDonald, Canadian Chief of the Canadian Nursing Sister Corps., was waiting to welcome us. This time we were packed two deep in waiting taxi-cabs with our luggage piled high on top. For most of us it was a first visit to old London and we were a curious lot, not talking much, but looking, as we travelled through the noisiest, busiest, narrowest, crowded streets one could imagine. It was so new, so interesting. I was in a daze trying to take it all in, and could not. We were billeted at the Kingsley Hotel in Bloomsbury Square, not far from Buckingham Palace and the British Museum, and I wondered "Can this possibly be me, or am I having a vivid dream?"

A good night's sleep in a real bed, breakfast, and we were off on a sight-seeing tour. Did you ever hear of the sight-seeing Colonials? Well, that was us! First, we visited the British Museum, which was within a stone's throw of our billets. I could scarcely tear myself away from the Art Gallery. I just wanted to stand and drink it all in. There were many large, bare spaces on the walls where famous and valuable pictures had been taken down, and hidden under sand bags for safety's sake in case of an air raid - pictures that could never be replaced. The sculpture was breathtaking, with exhibits from different corners of the earth. It was an education done up in a small parcel. There was little time to absorb it all and I promised myself a return visit when I could browse to my heart's content. Reluctantly we turned and left the building.

As we stood waiting for one of the Nursing Sisters, an old woman came along, and stood looking us up and down as if we might have been one of the Egyptian mummies of the Museum. She stepped up to Sister Prichard, the smallest and meekest of the party. "Excuse me please, but are you police women?" Not such an outrageous inquiry, considering our colorful navy blue uniforms with scarlet and white trimming, and scarlet-lined capes. To say nothing of the brass buttons decorating our fronts, and the Canadian Insignias on our epaulettes of which we were so proud... Police Women indeed!

Turning to the leaves of my old diary, I found that on May 15th, 1915 I had my first glimpse of the land of my forebears and wrote;

"Starting for France - we took the train to Folkestone. One never wearies of looking at the beautiful English countryside, the green, green grass, beautiful trees, and tiny canals with quaint barges drawn by sleepy looking old dobbins plodding along the banks. Every tree and thatched cottage seems to have been placed there purposely to create a picturesque landscape. The English coaches are very comfortable, even if the lace head-rests (tidies) looked a bit archaic. These trains travel at such a speed, things just sort of flash past-we never go up a grade; we hear a whirr and everything is black. Without any warning we fly through a small tunnel and in another moment we are travelling through a paradise of trees, with yellow flowers carpeting the ground beneath.

We went on board the *Victoria* heading for France, passing several torpedo destroyers in the English Channel. They guard the shores and give us a feeling of security at the same time. It was raining when we arrived at Boulogne at 7 p.m. The rain did not make matters any more cheerful. Red Cross ambulances were waiting for us and we noticed that rows and rows of these lined the wharf. This was an entirely new experience for all of us, and once more we were tightly packed two by two, into seats facing each other. There seemed to be soldiers everywhere - French, British, Canadian. I wondered if the Canadians did not look just a trifle trimmer than the others or if I was just prejudiced. The French private's uniform is a very sloppy, baggy affair, his scarlet trousers tucked in under the boot tops. The navy jacket, or tunic, is cut swallow-tailed style, or folded back to give that effect. White braid trimming extends down the sides of the legs. Add to this a round, sharp-peaked blue cap, and the combination made a rather picturesque outfit, reminding me of the pictures of the Confederate soldiers' uniforms during the American Civil War. Boulogne was a very dingy-looking town. Most of the women seemed to be wearing black dresses. The Louvre, where we were billeted, was also very dirty-looking, dingy and dusty. However, the food was much better than the appearance of the place would indicate. On our arrival we were served a hot dinner. So far our command of the French language was very limited. The majority of us could not even read the menu cards, so we ordered the whole works. What a display of food there was, and no rationing about it!

With all the excitement of the previous week, sleep simply would not come, and I surely had a lost feeling. We must have been near a station, for throughout the night, long trains passed to and fro. Later, we learned that these were the trains moving the troops up to the front. I wondered once more "Just what am I facing?" Possibly every newly landed woman or man had the same feeling. It was all so out of keeping with our peaceful way of living. In the evening many ambulances had passed on their way to the wharf, or up over the West Hill to No. 2 Canadian Stationary Hospital. A few months before I was so afraid that the war would be over before I even reached France. I had much to learn. I had not yet even touched the edge of this hideous, desperate war. Boulogne was peace. The day was to come when I would stand in a improvised hospital in the middle of a wheat field, and with eyes smarting with tears of resentment, view the victims of war, with a burring hatred of the very name of war in my heart.

After reporting and roll call, we were told that, for the time being, we were to be divided into groups and loaned to the established Imperial hospitals, until our units from Canada would arrive and receive us. In the meantime we were all to remember that we were in the army, and were willing to do whatever might be asked of us, without comment, as any good officer should. Along with eleven other Nursing Sisters, I was slated for Versailles and British No. 4 General Hospital. The other sisters were divided between Rouen and Wimereux. With our baggage, plus baskets of sandwiches (very small, oblong loaves of French bread, absolutely void of butter or mustard, split in half with thick slices of meat placed between) we boarded the train for Paris. The coaches were similar to those in England. At intervals, as we travelled along, we would see French soldiers standing on guard - truly we were at war. Upon reaching Etaples we could see that it was crowded with soldiers, mostly English, and several Canadian Nursing Sisters from No.1 Canadian General Army Hospital. Even at that early date Etaples had become a very large hospital base.

France looked very much like Canada, with it's rolling countryside and abundance of green trees. There seemed to be few fences, but rather low hedges and low stone walls. Just outside of Etaples a trainload of Belgian soldiers stood waiting on a siding, quite close to where our train had stopped for a few moments. The men were all hanging over the half doors of the train. They called to us, wanting to know if we were English. When we told them we were Canadian, we could hear, repeated all the way down the line, the surprised "Ah, Canadians". These soldiers were much trimmer than the French soldiers, especially the officers. Their uniforms resembled our air force uniforms, but were a greener shade of khaki.

We arrived at Paris at 1:30 p.m. and were taken for foreigners of some sort or other, possibly because our unfamiliar uniforms made us quite conspicuous. At any rate, we were foreigners in a foreign land, and a bit embarrassed by the stares. Afterward we were told we were the first Canadian Nursing Sisters to have arrived at that destination. It was all so new to us; the people, the noise, the hurrying to and fro, and the people of all description, from the smartly dressed to the peasant class. All along one wall, seated on a bench was a horde of refugees. We wondered who they were, why they were there, and where they were going. Just by looking at them you could almost feel the air of dejection. There were no laughing faces, and very few smiles.

The streets of Paris appeared to be so narrow and old, and the buildings so high. Chattering people on every side created confusing noise to our unaccustomed ears. Once more we had to wait for orders, but finally we were all set. We were to board a tram for Versailles- tram sounded so English. We seemed able to pick up different expressions that were new to us in this part of the world, depot and tram among them, much more quickly than we became acquainted with the monetary system. Pence, shillings, crowns, and guineas were all so confusing for me at first. I usually despaired trying to figure it all out and would simply hold out a handful of the unfamiliar coins, telling vendors to help themselves, helplessly trusting to their honesty. We were very glad to find the French money less complicated and even similar to our own.

At the Versailles station there was no one to meet us, and it was growing quite dark. Not being used to the ways of war we wondered what had gone amiss. Had there been a mistake? After a huddled conference we called the hospital, and gave a sigh of relief when we saw the ambulance arrive to pick us up. We were delivered to the billets of the Imperial Nursing Sisters. As we stood waiting there we could hear passersby discussing us. "Canadians I believe, let us go and have a look at them". Surely they must have been disappointed to find that we were not wearing feathers and carrying tomahawks.

It was our first night in the bedroom of a better class French hotel. It was the Vatel Hotel and typically French. Our rooms, on the fourth floor, were well furnished, with numerous ornate mirrors placed anywhere that they would fit. The place was beautifully clean, bright and airy. Everything seemed to be so peaceful, it was hard to believe that only a few miles away a war was raging. We knew that this step was only temporary, and that this grandeur would not go on for the duration of the conflict. After all the hectic weeks of preparing to leave Canada, crossing the ocean, our initial stay in London and the Conference at the Canadian Nursing Sisters Headquarters, we were all very happy that the morrow would bring some real work.

With the first rays of the morning sun peeping in at my window I opened my eyes and looked at my watch - 6 a.m. Then I listened-what was that slip-slop, rhythmical sound? Quietly hopping out of bed and looking out of the window I could see, down below on the cobblestone road, a battalion of French soldiers, out on route march, I presumed. They lacked the quick sharp step of the Canadian soldiers, but even so, they made an interesting picture, swinging along in their navy blue and scarlet uniforms, under the arch of the overhanging trees. The morning sun made splashes of colour along the way. I also watched an old man on the opposite side of the street, who looked as if he might have stepped out of a storybook. He wore a long yellow smock, that reached to just above his knees, wide black trousers, and a wide, black felt hat with a wide brim adding the finishing touch to the whole picture. He was using a long pole to turn off the street's carbon lights, one by one. The "old lamp lighter" in person.

Dressing quickly and going downstairs with my diary in my hand, I found, at the back of the hotel, a small garden enclosed by a low stone wall and almost covered by vines with clusters of pink flowers. Large tub-like containers held well-trimmed shrubs. With the branches of the huge trees overhanging the wall, this seemed an inviting spot to have afternoon tea or coffee. Several of the servants came out to have a look at this foreigner intruding so early in the morning. I smiled and said "Bonjour". That much I remembered from school days. Suddenly, with the onslaught of French words thrown at me, any French I had ever attempted to learn took wings. It was useless; all I could do, like any other foreigner, was just sit and feel and look stupid. However, thanks to a trace of French blood, dating from my Huguenot ancestry, I surmounted the difficulty with an eloquent up-lifting of my hands, palms outward, and a true French shrug of the shoulders. In the days to come this helped me over many an awkward spot. When the rest of the Sisters appeared a half hour later for breakfast, we were surprised to have the waiter usher us, not into the dining-room, but down several flights of steps to a dingy basement, along with the maids and chauffeurs.

Chapter One; Editor's Notes

1) The Hesperian (10,920 tons) was sunk by a submarine, 85 miles SW of the Fastnet on September 4th, 1915. Thirty-two lives were lost.

2) Sister Peggy Smith (Margaret Heggie Smith) lived at 173 Slater Street, Ottawa. She was born in Ottawa, May 24th, 1872, and had served in South Africa, 1902.

3) Sister Cooke (Helen Beryl Cooke) was born in Ottawa, April 19th, 1885.

4) The Lusitania (30,396 tons), the Pride of the Cunard Line, was sunk by a German submarine on Friday, May 7th, 1915. The official loss of life was 1,198 souls.

5) Matron Margaret Clotilde MacDonald (1879-1948) was Canada's most senior Military nurse. She had served in the Spanish-American War (1898), and one of eight Canadian Nurses sent to the Boer War (1899-1902). She also worked during the construction of the Panama Canal. MacDonald joined the Canadian Army Medical Corps in 1906. In 1914 she was put in command of the Canadian Nursing Service and went Overseas with the First Contingent.

6) Sister Prichard (Mae Alice Prichard) was born in Toronto, March 7th, 1880.

7) The Number Two Canadian Stationary Hospital went Overseas in 1914. At first it was located on the Salisbury Plain (October-November), then was sent to Le Touquet, France in November 1914, the first Canadian Unit to see service on the Western Front. Its original members are the only Canadians entitled to the 1914 Star. From October 1915 until April 1919 it was located at Outreau, France.

Chapter Two

France

To our delight we found that the hospital was the Trianon Palace, a short distance down the street from the Hotel Vatel. With hearts beating a little faster than normal we set out to commence our first day "on active service somewhere in France." We walked down a long avenue of trees, each trimmed to resemble a huge green vase. Entering through a wrought iron gateway, we faced our new home. The place was alive with soldiers in khaki, or hospital blues. Officers scurried here, there and everywhere. Several of the Imperial Nursing Sisters were also there, dressed in demure gray uniforms, white aprons and over-shoulder gray flannel, with scarlet bordered capes. Some wore scarlet capes. These were the Queen Alexandra's Imperial Nursing Sisters. Many of these sisters had served in British Military hospitals in India. Those in gray with scarlet borders were the Territorials, or regular British Military Nursing Sisters. As these Imperial Sisters passed by us they neither glanced at us nor wished us a good morning. Being essentially feminine I could not help glancing down at our own smart, light blue service uniforms, and feel a wave of pride that I was a Canadian

Going up the wide steps leading to two glass entrance doors we entered an elaborately decorated rotunda. There were large oil paintings hanging on the walls and heavy, richly colored draperies at the windows. To the right we could see, through the double glass doors, rows and rows of cots, occupied with newly arrived patients from the front line. What amazed me was the silence of the place. A burly Sergeant Major escorted us to the second floor and the Matron's office. It was a very small office with a huge desk, behind which sat a slightly-built elderly woman wearing a scarlet cape. The lady did not lift her head from her work to offer us a greeting. After several moments of what was becoming an embarrassing silence the Matron looked up and, I vow, through each one of us with the bluest, coldest eyes I ever hope to look into, and asked "Just who are you". We had chosen Sister Jones, an English girl, to represent us. In a very quiet, dignified manner she stated who we were and what we represented. We were really very proud of her. Then this very superior lady informed us that she never would consider us her Nursing Sisters. She criticized our uniforms and as well as she could she implied that we were inferior. I could feel my Scotch-Irish temper burn right down to the toe of my Canadian army boots. With a final warning that she would not let us on her hospital floors until she had interviewed some "higher up", we were ordered back to our billets, and she swept out of the room like a duchess, this Q.A.I.M.N.S. Back to our billets we all trotted to await our doom, and to work off our indignation. This soon evaporated with peals of laughter. Thank goodness for a Canadian sense of humour. We thanked our lucky stars that we were *not* one of the lady's Nursing Sisters. That was the last time we ever saw this very superior person while we were at the Trianon Palace. Two hours later an orderly came with a list of wards that we were to report to - we must have passed muster. I was placed on the third floor under a Territorial Nursing Sister, with a Voluntary Aid Detachment (V.A.D.), as our assistant. There were many times when I wondered just what use that V.A.D. was! If she had confined herself to washing utensils and setting up instrument trays, she might have been a help. As an assistant at a dressing, she was hopeless.

When we arrived at No. 4 British General Hospital, which had been in operation for about a week, the place was still elaborately outfitted as a fashionable hotel, formerly used for entertaining celebrities visiting France. Turning to my old diary I found that I had not given an accurate description of this famous place in France. The Trianon Palace was a large structure of white brick, four stories high. Typical of most French architecture it was extremely decorative. The many windows, or shall I call them doors, opened out into small verandahs with black wrought iron railings of the most intricate design. They served as windows as well as doors. They overlooked the vast grounds, dotted with many beautiful shrubs, trees and tennis courts. The interior was even more interesting. Long, spacious corridors ran down the centre of each level. The covering on the floor where I worked was of the softest rose and gray-blue carpet. Into this my feet sank at every step. At the end of the hall, wide double glass doors opened onto a large balcony overlooking the vast grounds. At some distance, but clear to the eye's view, could be seen the opening in the woods where, earlier, the Germans had fired their gun, the "Big Bertha". It was here also that they were stopped on their advance toward Paris.

On the other side of the corridor were the bedrooms. Each room had its own private bathroom finished in French marble of various colours, to match the room's decorative scheme. These rooms were really unique. The walls were papered in rich, elegant design. For example, one had a cream background with an overall pattern in delft blue, of quaint, old fashioned French ladies in frilled dresses and poke bonnets, seated in basket-like traps drawn by pudgy ponies over an artistic bridge. They meandered all over the walls. The heavy drapes or draw curtains at each window had exactly the same colouring and design as those of the walls, and were held back on either side by enormous silk ropes with long tassels in a matching blue. Again, as in the Hotel Vatel, we found mirrors in every conceivable spot, in all sizes, from full length to hand mirrors. Each room had its own unique colour scheme. We were fortunate to have arrived in time to see all this grandeur before it was dismantled and turned into a proper hospital.

On returning to our billets for dinner, we were amused to find that we had been transferred to the ball room. The Colonel of the hospital, on hearing where the Canadian Nursing Sisters had been asked to dine, had interviewed the hotel management and gone to some trouble to inform them that we were not only Nursing Sisters but also officers of the Canadian Army. When he had thus protested, he was informed that, as we were only nurses, in France we would be considered in the servant class, so we had been placed where we belonged, in the basement. With, I imagine a French shrug, and a lifting of his hands he had said "Oui, Oui" and dismissed the subject. Taking no chances he transferred us from the basement to the ball room. Here, under a crystal chandelier, a long table had been laid for us. For the present at least we would dine in state. One might say from the "ridiculous to the sublime".

Our work at No. 4 British General proved to be very interesting in many ways. On the fourth day after our arrival, much to our delight, we were slated for night duty, each in charge of a ward, with no V.A.D. Our night supervisor was a Q.A.I.M.N.S., a most charming woman, efficient and considerate in every way. We were all very happy as our work was running smoothly along. The patients were all surgical cases. In my ward I had a number of amputation cases, some having suffered the

Trianon Palace.

loss of both legs and arms. It was amazing how cheerful all these maimed men were. For them the war was over and they would be going back home to their own people. We found the work much different from what we had done in hospitals back home in Canada. There were what we called "dirty cases", where infection had set in owing to the men having lain for hours in the muddy trenches before being picked up by the stretcher bearers. Usually, by the time that they had reached the base hospitals, following an amputation at the Casualty Clearing Station, gas gangrene had developed. Now, without any doubt, gas gangrene carries the most horrible malodorous "smell" anyone could imagine. It was in the air, it saturated our clothing and hair. Once having smelled gas gangrene one could never forget it.

In order to clear up gas gangrene and prepare for the final operation, surgically cleaning the infected area and covering the stump with healthy skin, the Murphy-drip method was used. In containers elevated over the wounded area, a solution of saline or eusol was usually used. This extended to the stump by a long rubber tube, with an adjustable clip, tightened so that a drop at a time of the solution fell on the raw flesh. The solution was kept at a comfortable temperature and necessitated carefully watching. I often marvelled at how quickly a dirty, purulent wound became clean under this treatment. Then came the final operation and the patient was off to England. The war was over for them and they were happy, but at what a price. In 1915 we did not have the help of antibiotics to combat infection.

One unforgettable day the first "gassed" patients were admitted. These were pitiful, frustrating cases, many Canadian boys among them. This was an entirely new kind of warfare - horrible, and contemptible. We were at sea as to how to treat them or give relief. Even oxygen was of little help. Most of the men were gasping for breath from the searing of their throats and lungs. It was a terrible experience for the men and for those trying to help them. Later, this problem was conquered and we did learn how to give help and relief.

We were not long at No. 4 British General when the draperies and carpets were removed, much to everyone's satisfaction. Only the mirrors remained. Everything was spotlessly clean. The work of an efficient staff of well trained orderlies insured that everything was running like clockwork.

Night Duty

When I went on duty the first night, I received my night orders from Sister Taylor, the day sister in charge. Along with the many orders, she gave me a list of names and informed me that these fifty patients were to be ready for evacuation at 5 a.m. the following morning. With the many dressings to be done, twenty or more foot and arm baths to be watched, the comfort of the patients to be looked after, a poor little lad with a ghastly back wound whose position must be frequently changed, and several operative cases coming out of anaesthetic, I thought, "It just cannot be done". As my Irish grandmother might have suggested, "I put a button on my lip", and awaited developments.

At midnight, leaving the orderly in charge, I went down with the sisters for dinner, "in the bunk" as the Imperial Sisters called it. In the small breakfast room on the main floor we found the table centered with a huge bowl of red roses, a gift to the Canadian Nursing Sisters from Elinor Glyn, the naughty author who dared to write what she wished. Every day she came into Paris from her country home with an armful of flowers for the patients. Sister Ross, a rosy faced Scottish girl from Edmonton, Alberta, who had charge of the first floor, where the most critical patients were lying, came in late. Usually Scottie had a joke for us. This night her face had a tight expression, and even her veil seemed to hang at half mast. "Girls this war is hell, such wrecks of young manhood, just laddies!" She dropped her head on her out-stretched arms, and sobbed. We did not try to comfort her, we under-stood, and her tears relieved the tension.

Back on my ward the hours were creeping on to the dreaded 5 a.m. and my first evacuation. I had not counted on the efficiency of my well trained Imperial orderly. Much to my surprise, I found that by 4 a.m. our dressings were all completed, and most of the outbound patients ready and waiting for the stretcher bearers. The work had been accom-plished quickly and quietly and there was less confusion than one might find in a civilian hospital with the discharging of half a dozen patients. It was rewarding work, just to see the happy faces of these boys going back home to Blighty, looking forward to the trip on the hospital barges, that carried them part way to meet the train. These in turn met the boats at Boulogne wharf. Some of these men, when fully recovered, would return to France and their regiments; for others, they had done their part!

Even at this early stage, in the spring of 1915, the war seemed to have settled down into a steady business. So much hard work, so much suffering, so much red tape each day, and also so much pleasure. And with it all came such comradeship. The Canadians were looked on as subjects of curiosity. We were called the "Millionaire Colonials" owing to the fact that we were paid the magnificent sum of four dollars and ten cents a day. Perhaps it was hard for the old country people to under-stand our spontaneous personalities but we found it hard to penetrate their reserve. Even our expressions and ways of thinking and speaking were so entirely different. One diminutive English Medical officer got under my skin. Each round he would have some personal remark to make. Perhaps it would be "So, you are two stars up?" or "Why do you wear the Sam Brown belt?" I withstood it for several nights, trying to believe the little Major did not really mean to be rude. Feeling that I had answered enough questions one evening, I turned to him and quietly replied "Major Reilly, this is the Canadian Army Medical Corps uniform, I am proud of it and trying very hard to be worthy of wearing it." The fussy little man, whom one of the Canadian sisters called "the feather duster," blustered and apologized. Never again did he make a personal remark, he was courtesy personified from then on.

This war with all its rules was an entirely new experience for all of us. How should we act; what should we say, either on or off duty, and especially to outsiders? Evidently we were always under supervision, told where we should go and what was out of bounds for the military. It seemed sometimes the rule to follow was walk straight, salute your superiors, ignore the lowly private .... all a bally nuisance to most of us. It aroused our tempers. The rule at all times was to keep under control. Sister Terry was a French Canadian from Montreal, a daughter of one of the city fathers. Terry was lovely to look at, tall and dignified, with a wonderful poise. She resented very much everything about our introduction to the army. Not being allowed to dine in the main dining room; put with the servants in the basement at the Hotel Vatel; the cool welcome by the Matron and Nursing Sisters. It was entirely too much for Terry's pride to withstand. To relieve her feelings she sat down and wrote her father a long letter in French, telling him exactly what she felt about the whole affair. The Matron, how we were made to feel inferior - she covered reams of paper. But Terry had forgotten about the Camp Censor. One morning, coming off late duty, her head held high, walking very straight in her light blue uniform, always so immaculate, from the sheer folded veil to the toes of her shiny black army boots, cheeks flaming, and dark eyes blazing she announced, "Well, I am to be paraded before the O.C." She gave a chair a violent shove out of her way. "Now, what in hell does he want, whatever have I done that was wrong?"

"You mean that you are to be paraded before the Officer Commanding", we asked in unison, aghast.

"Yes" she snapped back, "Just that".

Hoping to relieve the tension, because together we always stood, we asked her if she had finished off the horrible old Major in the end bed, or forgotten his morning tea, or called the orderly "Dear", in His Highness' presence, "Or.. .." we went on helpfully. Before leaving to face her ordeal, she pulled off her veil and proceeded to fold a fresh one.

"Be sure to wear your sheerest white, remember Marie Antoinette for your execution" we suggested.

An hour later she came in, unaccompanied by any army guard. She sat down on the side of her bed, and started to laugh, while we stood around with our mouths open, waiting for the worst.

"Mon Dieu." Terry often reverted to her native tongue whenever she was excited or pleased. "Salute me, all you Canadian Nursing Sisters. Tonight I dine at the Ritz with the Colonel. He has decided that I am not actually a German spy, and forgiven me for the letter I wrote to my father in French! - I do hope that the censor knows!" she added, as she nestled under her blankets to dream of the coming dinner, without even a guilty blush for the contents of the letter she had written. Sister Terry was utterly guileless. Scottie too, snuggling under her blankets, shook her head "Now why couldn't I have thought of something like that?" She ruefully remembered what we would have for dinner that night.

One night while going on duty, I was delighted to find in one of the wards, four Canadian boys from Montreal. Up until then we had had very few Canadians. Feeling a little homesick, I could not keep my delight submerged, as the day Sister gave me the night orders.

Looking at me with a surprised expression, Sister Taylor remarked "How extraordinary, fancy making such a fuss over some Canadian Tommies". For once I regretted that I must hold my temper, be professional and maintain my dignity, because I knew that the very cream of Canadian men walked in the ranks. Nevertheless, the Montreal boys never lacked Canadian magazines, cigarettes or flowers while they remained at No. 4 General Hospital.

My First Zeppelin

It was the first night that my floor had boasted an empty bed. For some reason there were several. Around 4 a.m. everything was quiet, and I sat down to fill out my night report, day orders and history sheets. Sitting with my head bent over my work, I suddenly heard from overhead, a Zoom, Zoom! For a moment I turned cold. Through my mind ran the many accounts of the raids on England. With a start I wondered whatever I would do should the hospital be bombed. Being near the top of the building I felt sure that we would be the first to suffer. Quickly my mind ran down my wards on either side of the corridor. I thought "Most of the men are walking cases and can look after themselves, but what about little Jim?" Jim was a fifteen year old boy from London, who would never have been in the army, had his true age been known. He was now here, with both of his legs amputated above the knees. After he had been wounded, he had lain in a crater (a large hole in the ground torn up by a bursting shell) before he had been found and picked up by the stretcher bearers and carried out to safety. It had never occurred to me that I might be hit myself - I knew that I could carry Jim out, he was such a little fellow, so frail, so young.

As the zooming continued overhead, I was absolutely sure that it was a Zeppelin of the very worst type. The orderly passed my door, apparently undisturbed. Bitingly I thought "That nonchalant air of Watson's - just more British efficiency". Well, I would show him just how cool a Canadian could be under the circumstances. At the same time I could not still the rapid beating of my own heart. "Zoom! Zoom!" It was coming nearer and nearer. Unconsciously I lifted my eyes to the ceiling - there it was, the Zeppelin, a huge, downy white moth... My first air raid while on duty... somewhere in France. From sheer thankfulness and relief, I rose and walked the full length of the corridor to where Jim lay in the end room. He was sleeping peacefully, one hand tucked under his cheek, a mere infant. Pushing open the glass doors leading onto the balcony, I stepped out into the early morning air. Dawn was just breaking in the east. Peeping over the tree tops were the pink and mauve rays of the morning sunshine. The birds were fairly bursting their throats with song, such carolers! Oh, the music and the beauty and peace of it all. Overhead a bird with a marvellous trill of notes was losing itself in the fleecy clouds high, high up... a lark no doubt. From somewhere behind the trees the bleating of sheep could be heard, apparently a large flock, food for the French army. I stifled a sigh. What a lovely world to be caught in the throes of war. Could there be a God who would allow such tragedies as the injuries of little Jim? He had been only a morsel for the German guns to tear and wound. I remembered Doctor Middlebro's remark, "Fodder for the guns". Three doors from me lay such fodder. Two months earlier he had stood and looked up into a morning sky as lovely as this one. Now he lay broken and burned. It had been April 22nd, 1915 at St. Julien that the

Canadians had encountered the first gas attack. Early in the morning, over the parapets rolled the hideous greenish yellow vapor mist. It first burned their eyes, then their throats as they inhaled the foul stuff, coughing and confused and in an agony that water could not relieve. Had many heeded the quick thinking advice of a young chemist from Sarnia, Ontario, they might have found at least temporary relief. Recognizing the gas, he knew that it should be neutralized, but having nothing to work with, he suddenly thought of urine's alkaline content. He tried to advise as many around him as would listen. To some the cure was almost as repulsive as the gas. Those who listened and took his advice got relief, and finally reached the base hospital as my patient had done. There he lay, his face swollen and burned, his lungs filled with mucus and pus. The worst part of it was that the Medical Officers and Sisters did not know how to give relief and it broke our hearts. It was a terrible form of warfare, and Germany would forever carry the disgrace of introducing it. I loathed the enemy with all the hatred of which I was capable.

When the time for going off duty arrived, instead of going straight to the billets for breakfast as usual, I turned down the street leading to a wide boulevard, lined on either side with huge chestnut trees. The sweet, cloying perfume of the white blossoms on the branches spreading overhead was breathtaking. The sun was shining through the trees creating a network of yellow and brown shadows on the soft earth underneath; a fairy avenue of loveliness. A wave of homesickness came over me. There was something familiar about the scene, yet back home the trees would be wide spreading maples, and there would be a hill, with a wooden bridge at the foot of it. This was all very different. Stopping to take it all in, I saw approaching under the trees a French Cavalry out on route march. Prancing and tossing their heads, were lovely jet black and chestnut horses with shining coats. How proud they looked, as if trying to do justice to their riders who wore silver-plumed helmets that flashed like jewels, as patches of sunshine caught and threw back their glitter. Very dignified were the cloaks worn by each, as they rode along. When the wind stirred the cloaks were thrown back, displaying the scarlet linings underneath. I stood to one side to watch them go by. It was a gorgeous scene, and it was hard to believe that it was a part of warfare. I questioned again, "Why do wars have to come?" There seemed to be no answer.

"Souvenir, souvenir Canadien!" demanded two small boys, as I turned to retrace my steps. What darlings they were with their quaint pinafores of black sateen, gathered full on a deep yoke, and topped with a white Eton collar. Only by the short trousers would anyone guess that they were boys, especially the one with the thatch of black curls. I stood looking down at them, wishing with all my heart that I could talk to them. "Souvenir!" they demanded, pointing to my brass buttons and stars. Not even to please a dear little French boy could I part with my precious buttons.

I was weary. It had been a long hard night and my feet ached as I tramped along over the cobblestone road. As so often happened when we were out walking, I came face to face with a small company of French soldiers, trudging along, their backs laden with heavy equipment, singing as they marched. I winced when a heavy army truck with its steel wheels screeched past. What a fearful business it all was! Walking past the Imperial Nursing Sisters billets, I wondered if we would ever really get to know them. How strange when we were all working for the same cause, that we had so little in common. It was not until many months later, at a Casualty Clearing Station on the Somme, that I learned the truth of the warm natures hidden beneath the cold exteriors we were encountering every day.

There was no sleep for me that day it seemed. On returning to our billets I wondered at the commotion coming from our quarters. Opening the door I found the girls as wide awake as if they had slept all night, scurrying around, evidently preparing for some jaunt or another. My dress uniform was lying on the bed waiting for me.

I was greeted with "Hurry along, we are off to Paris!" A few uncomplimentary remarks were thrown in, about my wandering off on my own and keeping the family waiting. It would never have occurred to them to have gone on without me.

"But I saw such a wonderful sight, a French cavalry out on march!" I tried to explain, as I tuselled with my long black braids.

"Oh, step a la view (a lingo of our own) we have to catch a tram!", called our versatile Seely as she bustled around in preparation. "My hat please Walker!" I caught the hat as it was literally hurled in my direction.

"Merci", I said as I plunked it straight up and down on my head. Thanks to our dining-room maid we were becoming quite familiar with the French language. What we did not know when Marie was through with us would not be her fault.

It was a gorgeous day for an adventure. Soon we were all ready and packed into the open tram on our way to the famous old city of Paris. Someone better informed than the rest of us stated that we had better watch our "P's" and Q's", that in Paris anyone accidentally knocked down is fined for obstructing the traffic, rather than the fellow who had actually done the damage, and apparently there are fewer accidents there than in any other city in the world. Remembering that we had not yet received our army pay we decided to play safe by hiring a taxi as soon as we arrived at the depot.

Paris is such a beautiful city, and so interesting; not crowded or dense as we had found London. The love of beauty seemed to have been uppermost in its planning... or did it just grow? Plenty of space, trees and shrubbery, statuary and magnificent arches. Turning down the Champs Elysees, we were thrilled with its many trees and quaint lamp posts. In the distance we could see the Arc de Triomph, the wide bridge spanning the river Seine, the unique architecture of the buildings on either side of the Eiffel Tower, and the colourful garden and Monument to Gambetta. All of this made a very interesting tour. We got out to stand under the Arc de Triomph, to watch the people come and go. So many of the women seemed to be wearing black, with wide hats draped with black veils, varying in length from the shoulder to the hem of their skirts. Their costumes were very chic but a bit depressing. Then we realized that many of these women were in mourning for loved ones killed while on active duty. Later we learned that in France the veil is not always restricted to widows, but a sign of mourning in any case.

What the French women lacked in colourful dress the French officers made up for, with their natty gray-blue uniforms and the navy blue and crimson-lined capes. There seemed to be officers and French soldiers everywhere we turned. Perhaps the most interesting place we visited that day was the Column Vendome. Remembering my old Bible stories, told to me by my father I wondered if this could possibly be one of the Obelisks of Egypt where Mary and the Babe Jesus and Joseph had rested in the shadow of the Obelisk, on their way to Nazareth" "It must be", I pondered, but surely some changes must have been made. I knew that three Obelisks left Egypt, one for Paris, one for London and one for New York. I was still uncertain. Standing many feet high, topped with its peculiar Egyptian figure (a Sultan) it offered the irresistible temptation of going inside and climbing the many steps of the spiral stairway. Arriving at the top, almost exhausted for want of breath, we stood gazing out over the rooftops of the city and felt that the view from that vast height made the effort well worthwhile. In the distance we could see the glittering bronze statue of Joan of Arc, burnished golden by the sun.

Descending the stairway, we decided that it was time to leave for Versailles, if we were to have any sleep that day. First we went with Sister Seely, a devout Catholic, to Notre Dame Cathedral. Not much wonder that this is such a famous church, beautiful and dignified, with its lovely stained glass windows of intricate design. It was all so peaceful after the bustling world outside, we felt that it would be well to bow our heads in reverence and pray with Sister Seely. As we sat waiting in silence, from some remote choir loft came the most heavenly music. We listened until the last chord died away in the arches of the high ceiling. Leaving, we felt as if a benediction had been pronounced by someone unseen. An hour later we crawled into our beds, weary, but with our brains filled with the wonder of it all. I could not help wondering if I could possibly be the same girl from Owen Sound, Ontario, that little town so far away... sleep had come.

I came off duty on a morning in May, foot-weary and heartsore. The night had been a hectic one for in each bed lay a seriously wounded man. There had been little laughter that night. The reports brought in by the incoming patients had been very pessimistic, especially regarding the fighting around Hill 60, which had become a nightmare to us. Too many lives had been lost. How long was it going to last? How many more boys would have to say farewell to Canadian hillsides and freedom and become a mere part of a unit, following one creed, the word "Obey." Word had come from home that a schoolmate of mine had been killed in action somewhere in France. How sore his mother's heart must be, only one boy left and he already in training. I cried, yet had to laugh, as I tucked Mother's letter in my uniform pocket. I wondered just what idea she had of the whole affair. "Do be careful and try not to get yourself into a dangerous spot," she wrote. I looked up into the branches of the wide spreading chestnut tree. No doubt Mother thought I was sitting astride a parapet, or dodging bullets most of the time. How I longed for someone of the dear home people as I turned into the Petit Trianon Palace gateway and followed the winding path. We never tired of walking in these famous old grounds, with the soft green grass, flowering shrubbery and borders of roses. And there were hidden surprises. Perhaps a piece of marble statuary tucked away in a corner of ornamental bushes or an unexpected pathway. The miniature mill where Marie Antoinette played at being a dairy maid was now almost covered with vines; the lovecote of the same Marie; pathways running here and there in all directions. Poor little Marie, to have possessed all of this-to have lived, loved and laughed and in the end to have been trundled in an open cart through the streets, watched by a surging crowd - to meet a horrible death on the guillotine. So brave she had been to have dressed herself in her finest apparel and gone forward, with her head held proudly high. Perhaps my sympathies were more sincere owing to the fact that, back in the time of Marie Antoinette, ancestors of my own had fled from France to Ireland and safety.

Wandering around I found a small open field completely surrounded by tall trees. Peeping here, there and everywhere were scarlet poppies, the first that I had seen. A story had been told that Marie Antoinette, at one time, wished that poppies grew where she might go out and gather them, much as a Canadian girl might gather trilliums in the springtime. Antoinette had her wish gratified; poppy seeds were scattered in this small field behind the Petit Trianon Palace grounds. From the Palace, poppies spread far and wide, throughout France. I thought how pretty they were; the time had not yet arrived when I would close my eyes at the very sight of them. Walking on I came upon the quaintest of tiny French houses. I presumed it might be the home of one of the caretakers. Over the front door of the stone house, cream-coloured roses climbed almost to the roof, peeping in at the open, lead-pane windows. A chubby little Frenchwoman came out to greet me "Blesse oui?" With a sympathetic lift of her shoulders, she darted back into the house but soon appeared with a pair of large shears. She clipped rose after rose and laid them in my arms, patting them with a small white hand, "Blesse Anglais... Merci." I nodded, hugging the lovely things to myself, and turned to retrace my steps to my ward in Trianon Palace. Later, as I closed my eyes, I wondered if little Jim would he conscious enough to notice the bowl of roses by his bedside. Perhaps it might bring a spark of comfort to know they had been sent especially for him.

The following day was the Sabbath. "There will be Divine Service held on the grounds at 5 p.m. Sister Wilson, try to be there if possible," said the kindly, slightly-stooped Anglican Padre, as he turned to leave my ward. It seemed as if it had been months since I had attended a church service. True, we had attended a service in St. Paul's Cathedral, London. The ceiling seemed so high; the huge sounding board behind the speaker sent echoes here and there and as a result I could catch but very little of the sermon. I was very depressed and felt I needed assurance of some sort. Here was a man with soft gray eyes offering me that comfort. As I put on my sheerest white hemstitched veil and spotless apron in preparation for the evening service, my mind travelled across the ocean to my home town church. I was again in the old choir loft, slipping into my choir gown, adjusting my mortar-board cap. I could hear the organ in the distance. Soon we would be all filing up to take our places; sopranos, altos, basses, tenors. Ah! No it would not be the same, there would be fewer basses and tenors, most of them attending service in an army camp. And one alto would be attending Divine Service out under the tree of the Trianon Palace in France. It was a quiet group that took its place under the spreading branches, on Sunday evening. Groups of patients in the familiar gray hospital pyjamas, topped with a bright blue outer robe, sat in wheel chairs or on the ground. There was no talking; the thoughts of many would be with their home folk in the Colonies, England, Ireland or Scotland. Overhead the birds called softly to each other as the sun slid behind the trees in the west. Padre Millar stood up and announced the opening hymn, "Abide with me." Surely Jesus must have stood and listened, as that grand old hymn rose, with such sweetness and sincerity from the throats and hearts of those soldier boys. Again, in the most simple language, the Padre spoke of the Saviour's love, words of encouragement that we all needed so badly. He spoke of hope and entreaty to hold fast to our faith. I felt ashamed that so many times I had felt it difficult to hold fast and yet understand. In my heart a great comfort seemed to settle as I went on duty that night - I would try to understand.

Chapter Two; Editor's Notes

1) Elinor Glyn (1864-1943) was an English novelist who wrote highly romantic novels, from a woman's point-of -view. She was considered quite 'modern' in her attitudes.

2) Sister Seely (Eleanor Seely) was born in Petrolia, Ontario January 26th, 1885.

Chapter Three

A Pleasure Trip

One Sunday in late May we were all astir, looking forward to our first trip to St. Germain. Little thrills of anticipation chased themselves up and down my spine, for I was actually going to see the setting of my best loved novel, Les Miserables. Cosette and Jean Val Jean had been like real friends of my own.

The son of a wealthy resident of Versailles, kept out of the army by defective eye-sight, had placed his automobile and himself at the service of the patients and staff of No. 4 British General Hospital. I wondered why Sister Taylor's eyes danced when I told her of our plans for the afternoon. At 2 p.m. sharp a shining touring car, the top rolled back as far as possible so that no part of the scenery might be missed, stopped at our door. Seated at the wheel was a trim looking youth, wearing dark glasses, and dressed in a natty uniform of light blue. He assisted us to our places in the car. We might have been nobility, so extravagant were his attentions and courtly bows. Apparently, what he lacked in knowledge of the English language he made up for in courtesy. Off we started, and down the long boulevard, we actually whizzed. "Well" thought I, "for a man with defective eye-sight this is some speed." We all tried to remember how to say "Slow down!" in French. Sister Walker, who had the place of honour in the front seat and had been talking conversational French, now tried out all the words she could recall that might mean "slow down". It was useless. The gentleman only repeated "Oui, oui", and continued on his merry way, while those of us in the back seat clutched our navy hats with one hand and grasped anything handy with the other. We hoped that we might not slide off, or bounce clear into space, from the shiny, slippery black leather upholstering. The poppies were mere flashes of red, the trees streaks of green, as we tore along. After miles of the most frightening, bewildering speed we landed on the top of a hill overlooking a small village. It was the longest, steepest most twisting hill I had ever looked down, and I shuddered. Houses were built close together on either side of the cobblestone road. Only then did our driver slacken his pace enough for us to get a glimpse of the beautiful climbing roses that grew everywhere. With a pleased grin, he gave his shoulders a shrug and stated "Oui, oui St. Germain". On gaining the foot of the hill, we flew off again, while children, dogs and hens flew and scattered in all directions for safety. In five minutes we had flitted into and out of St. Germain. When I went on duty that night Sister asked "Have a pleasant afternoon? Drives like the devil doesn't he?" With all my heart I replied "Oui, oui!"

Sister Taylor ran down her list of orders for the night, medicines, dressings and evacuations. . . "And by the way the escort will be here at 6 a.m., see that the orderly has Scottie ready".

"Escort! Scottie?", I asked.

"Why yes, did you not know that private McDonald has been a war prisoner here for several weeks. The wound on his right hand was self inflicted. In the army that is a criminal offense," stated the sister matter-of-factly.

"Oh," was all I could say as, with a feeling of nausea, I thought of the slightly built Scottish boy, with his homely face and kind eyes, who sat day in and day out nursing a horribly wounded hand and talking to Paddy as if Paddy were his own special charge. Paddy, who would never walk again and whose endless days were made shorter by the quiet Scottish boy. "Scottie a prisoner!" It did not seem possible. As the small hours of the morning drew near, I looked in at Scottie, and saw that he was quietly dressing himself. I inspected each out-going patient, purposely leaving Scottie until the last. With a sinking feeling I went to his door.

"Your dressing Scottie please." As was his custom he sat on a high chair beside my dressing table. The wound was actually healed. As if he felt that he must right himself in my opinion, he told his pathetic story. He had always been partially deaf, but his companions were all joining the army, so he successfully bluffed his way past the recruiting officers. The long months of training passed, and eventually he reached the front trenches. His hearing became worse from the vibration of the guns, yet he hesitated about going to a Medical Officer for fear of being considered a shirker. He became more frustrated, then he said, "It was not actually all my fault. I just lost my head, and I did shoot off my trigger finger". He had been charged and he was to be court-martialled and, in all probability, sentenced.

"I will never be back Sister, please take care of Irish for me, and the other lads. God only knows how they appreciate it, how much it means to them." I shuddered as I saw a Sergeant and an armed private coming up the stairway - cruel war, and hateful. I sent up a silent prayer that the Officers judging Scottie would be kind and lenient.

It was to be a gala day at the Grande Palace. (In this building the Armistice would be signed). For one day the city of Paris was turning the fountains on full to raise money for the French soldiers. The cost was so great that only for very special occasions was this done. It was a beautiful Sabbath morning, so Sister Walker and I decided it would be a very good time to visit the Palace. All of Paris seemed to have turned out in full force. French Officers in dress uniforms, ladies beautifully costumed, children looking like butterflies or fairies in short, sheer, colourful dresses as they danced among the shrubbery and flower beds and the many white marble statues. It was almost unbelievably beautiful, so beautiful it is hard to describe the scene taking place that day. The Grande Palace is one of the most famous and important buildings in all of France. For this one day it was thrown open to the public, and only a small fee was charged. Going up the wide steps of the main entrance, you enter a very wide, almost square hall. On either side stand the statues of Louis XIV and Louis XV. To the left a gray marble stairway with several landings leads to the second floor. At the top of the first flight of steps, hangs a very large oil painting, "The Fete". The detail of this piece of work is so fine the perspective so perfect, that even the faces in the distance are as clear as photographs. One could almost imagine it a part of the immense crowd outside that very afternoon.

This proved to be only the beginning of the many gems to be found in the historical old building. It was easy to understand how the building with such magnificent architecture inside and out, gold-leaf decorating and precious paintings, had almost financially crippled France. It must have cost an immense sum of money.

Perhaps the most colourful and interesting room was the Battle Gallery. It was a long, expansive room, with great marble pillars placed at intervals along either side, and topped with busts of famous French soldiers. The walls between the pillars were covered with oil paintings of battles fought and won by Napoleon. There is only one way to describe these paintings, almost life size with incredible detail - they were overwhelming. The finishing touch was the soft overhead lighting that cast a glow over the entire scene, bringing out the delicate colouring of each picture.

Madame Pompadour's suite of rooms, or what was left of it, (we were told many very valuable pieces had been sold), gave one a small idea of what that giddy, influential Mistress must have been like. Very "French" and gay, with carved back chairs, elaborate drapes, oil paintings on the wall, the rich wood, many mirrors, and several tables and cabinets with designs in inlaid mother-of-pearl. It was all very beautiful.

The ballroom was quite the most beautiful, with its huge amethyst crystal chandeliers, hanging at intervals from the ceiling. The ceiling alone was unique, decorated with cupids and garlands of flowers in pastel shades. Here again, over the long row of French glass doors leading onto the small balconies, gold leaf decorating hung like gold lace festoons draped completely around the room from pillar to pillar. As we wandered from room to room, the fountains kept up a continuous music outside.

Directly at the foot of the main steps leading to the front entrance, the fountain, *Le Tapis Vert*, held a fascination for me. It was so entirely different from anything a person might expect to find in this exact spot and I decided it was rather ugly, with its group of bronze frogs shooting spouts of water ten to twelve feet in the air from gaping mouths. Just below this and to the right, lay one of the many rose gardens, a delight. The rose trees looked like so many huge umbrellas spread wide open, the top completely covered with roses of every shade, making the air fragrant with perfume. Among the rose trees were many small playing fountains, giving the whole place a misty aura. Standing as we were, facing the western sun, they looked like so many rainbows. Descending the steps, we walked down a wide pathway with green boulevards on either side, flanked with tall white statues at intervals of perhaps ten or fifteen feet. At the very foot of the walk was the centre of the pool. It was hard to realize amid all this grandeur that only a few short miles away great guns were playing on human beings. Things seemed to be all out of proportion. Here, peace and beauty;

there, horror, confusion and death. Little did we know, as we walked back to our billets to prepare to go on duty, that this would be the last night we would spend in Versailles. Just before going off duty the following morning, movement orders came for all Canadian Nursing Sisters to return to their own units and hospitals. Looking back, Versailles had been an interesting experience. In fact, we felt we had been especially favoured to have been sent to No. 4 British General Hospital. Now we were entering an entirely new adventure.

Duty in a Canadian Unit

Dusk was falling when we drew into Etaples depot and climbed into the waiting ambulances which were to take us to No. 2 Canadian Stationary Hospital at Le Touquet. We were to remain there for the night and wait for further orders. The most pleasant and welcome sounds to be heard were the Canadian voices on all sides. There was not one objection made, even in an undertone, when we were ushered into a large marquee, with the name over the door, "Montreal". The French Canadians were effervescent in their delight. With true Canadian hospitality we were welcomed by the Matron and Sisters as their guests. Before retiring for the night we went for a stroll. As we waited to let an ambulance pass through the gateway we were surprised to see, sitting beside the driver, a small boy of five or six years, looking like a miniature Canadian soldier in his khaki uniform, peaked cap and brown curls framing his baby face. He was all smiles as he saluted along with the driver. We wondered to whom he belonged. Later we were told that he had been picked up by some British soldiers on the retreat from Mons. He had been too small to give them any information. He was simply lost and sobbing his heart out, so they took him along with them and some Canadians had more or less adopted him.

That retreat from Mons held a mystery. I had been given many different versions but never by one who had actually participated in the event. The first and most often told.... The Germans were advancing, when they saw coming over the hill a large army, so they turned and fled. Many people had left their homes fearing an invasion of the German army. The little boy had become separated from his people and become lost, and had been picked up by the British soldiers returning with some wounded. He had finally wound up at No. 2 Canadian Stationary Hospital at Le Touquet. Here he had found a happy home and refuge, and for the time being he had become their mascot. He was learning the English language rapidly and being petted and spoiled by Sisters and men as well. We wondered what would become of him eventually. However, a Canadian officer was hoping that if all efforts to locate his own people failed, he could adopt him and take him back to Canada.

The Retreat from Mons or "The Angel of Mons" - recently I read this story of the Retreat from Mons, presumably told by an old soldier of the Old Contemptibles. This is an amazing story, and I am still bewildered. This soldier's regiment was at Mons when the retreat order was given. For some unknown reason the Germans were given the same order. It was a misty morning when the British regiment started to fall back, eventually coming to a dense forest, a tactical dead end. While they debated whether or not to divide, one half going in one direction, the other half in the opposite, there appeared out of the mist an angel, in a cloud, beckoning them to follow. This they did, and, reminiscent of the Bible story of the dividing of the Red Sea, they found a road and passed through safely. To this day that road has never been found.

Early the following morning, orders came for us to report to No. 1 Canadian General, a one-thousand bed hospital at Etaples. Driving back east through Paris Plage, we passed through a large town of canvas tents, hundreds of large square marquees and rows of bell-shaped tents. Passing a German Internment camp we could hear both laughter and music. Evidently they were enjoying their prison camp life away from the trenches, and being well cared for. Large, burly fellows, their uniform caps giving their head and features an unattractive appearance, it was not much wonder the boys called them bullet-heads. To us they were simply "Huns" and we wasted little time on them. We also passed a detention camp. There was neither music nor laughter to be heard from those quarters and it gave me a feeling of revulsion and loathing, to think what war can do to humiliate men. Many of their crimes would be treated as jokes in civilian life. Crimes such as over-stepping late leave, then trying to sneak in over the back fence. This of course is only one of the lesser crimes. There must be discipline in the army, strict discipline; soldiers are not all angels. At the same time it is cruel, something that has to be confronted, withstood and survived.

Arriving at No. 1 Canadian General, we reported immediately to the Matron's office, for our orders. Once more we were welcomed with a friendly handshake, and we felt that this time we were not a misdirected package. Here too I received my first army post of honor. The other sisters were dismissed, and under the charge of a Sister from Kingston, Ontario, were introduced to our sleeping quarters before going on duty on the wards. Our first home under canvas! In the meantime I was enlightened as to why I had been asked to remain. After several very direct questions, regarding my past training in Canada, I was told that I was being placed on duty as Night Supervisor. Outwardly I do not think I appeared to flinch, but down inside I was one big question mark, "Can I do it?. Supervise a thousand-bed hospital, when I do not know the Administrative building from the morgue!" There was one comforting fact; I was to work under the retiring Night Supervisor for three nights, to learn the ropes. So my spirits rose somewhat.

The following three nights were busy ones, as I learned the lay of the land and the various wards. There were the Operating room, X-Ray room, and the Administration Building, with all its offices. Night reports had to be made out each morning, supplies ordered for the different wards, and various other duties that were a part of carrying out the work of the Night Supervisor. I almost decided that she should actually be called the red tape Supervisor. I was working with fully trained nurses, who knew their work and did it well. With their splendid co-operation my work was made easy and I enjoyed every minute, hoping that I might be left there for the duration. Alas, in the army such a hope is often only wishful thinking.

On the third night I was awakened by the rain pattering on the canvas roof of my tent, a very small, buff-coloured canvas that resembled an Indian wigwam. The large canvas marquees were square with wooden floors; the outside wall made of drab canvas with an inner lining of buff orange. So the inside was protected from rain or wind. Each marquee held from forty-seven to fifty beds, with usually a small service space partitioned off for the Nursing Sisters' equipment, history sheets and records. It was my first night strictly on my own as Supervisor with all the responsibility resting on my young shoulders. Few would have guessed how young I felt. I prayed the dear Lord would help me, for I needed help very badly. I prayed that I might be worthy and that I would not make a mess of things in general.

The rain continued to play a tattoo overhead. "Well, no marble walls or halls for me tonight," I mused, as I pulled on my long rubber boots, fastened up my raincoat with it's flapping rubber cape, pulled down my souwester, and started out with the hope that I might not lose my way in the maze of canvas marquees. I had visions of finding myself wandering down the wards of the St. John's Ambulance Hospital, or one of the other Imperial hospitals... that surely would give the impression of inefficiency on the part of a Canadian Nursing Sister. The rain was coming down in torrents and there was a very high wind. "What a night!" I thought, when at last I turned up the wick of my round, "perfection" oil stove. Several times I had actually lost my way in the darkness and had had to take to one of the wards to reorient myself. The most annoying thing about the whole procedure was that I kept tripping over the guy ropes holding the tents down, once finding myself sitting in the soft mud. This was very hard on the temper and the dignity as well. At least no one could hear my inward blastings, let it be said to my credit.

My last task before going off duty, and reporting to the Matron's office, was to waken the day staff at six a.m. Picking up a small stick I walked over a small hillock and gently tapped on the first canvas hut. "Right" came a decidedly English voice, so on to the next.

"Is it really seven o'clock?" asked a second English voice. From hut to hut, I never missed a single call. British voices replied. "Where in the name of goodness did Canada pick up so many English Nurses?" I wondered. I could hear angry groans and enquiries regarding the time of day from one hut to another. It suddenly occurred to me that I was in the wrong camp, and I sped over another small hillock and came to a more familiar surrounding, thinking at the same time "This is no place for me." I crept quietly away and left them to figure out for themselves the correct time of day, and then turn over for another hour's sleep. I took a good look at the occupant of the next tent, to make sure that she was an honest-to-goodness Canadian - and made no more mistakes that morning.

I never wearied of the view from No. 1 General hospital, especially in the early morning. I tried to time my last visit for the observation marquee that stood on a hillside a short distance from the main hospital. There infectious and doubtful cases were held until properly diagnosed. The view looked west over the buff coloured city of tents and marquees, through the green trees, to the village of Paris-Plage with its red roofed building adding a touch of colour. Off the lighthouse, the many small fishing smacks lay waiting for the incoming tide. It was all breathtaking. The only jarring note at this hour of the morning was the long line of gray ambulances, each with a red cross on either side, slowly winding their way up the incline with the wounded patients from the early morning trains, so many for the Imperials, so many for the Canadian hospitals. Still overhead the birds poured forth a merry morning song. So weary was I when coming off duty that I was always ready to crawl into my army cot, and sleep the sleep of the just until 6 p.m.

My stay at No. 1 General was all too short. One afternoon at about 4 p.m. I was called and told to make haste and dress and be ready to take the 5 p.m. train to Boulogne, and from there, the following morning, a boat to England. "Poor me, whatever have I done to be recalled to England?". My heart was in my boots, and I knew I had tried so hard to carry out my duties well and faithfully. There was nothing for it but to pack once more, and leave the tiny tent that I had come to love. With hurrying fingers I dressed, packed my steamer trunk, hold-all and dunnage bag, and then went to report to the Matron's office to hear the worst. My orders were to report to the Matron-in-Chief's office in London. Under my charge were to go all the French Canadian sisters, who were returning to join their own unit somewhere near Paris. Along with the Nursing Sisters from Montreal and Quebec City, I crawled, bag and baggage, into the waiting ambulances. As we passed the Sisters' mess hut we could hear the bugler calling them all to come and dine. Where to now? Would I ever see France again, I wondered?

Chapter Four

Off For Fields Far Away

We spent the night at the Louve Hotel in Boulogne. It had not improved, either in cleanliness or appearance, since the last time we had been there. Sometime during the night I was wakened by someone outside my window giving sharp military orders. I got up quietly and leaned out. There in the square below, soldiers were crowded, full equipment packs on their backs. A gentle rain was falling as it did so often in those days in France. I knew the soldiers were new arrivals from the boats and England. The officer was speaking in a low voice, so I could not hear what he was saying. The men stood quietly listening and waiting. Then, at a sharp command, they formed fours and marched across the bridge and up the long hill. Once more I recalled Doctor Middlebro's remark, "More food for cannon". Now I knew how true it was. I wondered if they were Canadians. A great lump rose in my throat. "Poor boys whoever they are". To how many of them was this merely an adventure? How many would never return? Ah, how soon that great adventure would become a grim reality amid the horrors that awaited them. I had learned in the few months that I had been nursing in France what war really was.

The following morning we boarded the *Victoria* on our way back to England. I hunted for a seat on the upper deck where I could wrap myself in my steamer rug and remain until we reached Folkestone. I had no desire to walk around or do any sight-seeing as I recalled my last sea-sick crossing, when the waters seemed to toss the small boat forward and back and sideways, all at the same time. There was little delay in Folkestone after the disembarking vouchers were attended to. We went immediately aboard the waiting train, and were soon travelling toward London. Again I wondered if I would ever again write home with the heading "On active duty, somewhere in France". I was afraid of being placed in some beautiful home hospital, when I wanted so desperately to be working somewhere near the front. Little did I know how fortunate I was. Arriving at the Kingsley Hotel I was surprised to find the place fairly buzzing with Canadian Nursing Sisters, among them some of the girls I had not seen since crossing the Atlantic. I was more than pleased to find a particular friend, who until then had been on duty at Westgate Hospital, Eye, Ear and Throat, in England.

For the first time since leaving Etaples, France, my mind was at rest as I learned that I had been recalled to join my own No. 3 Canadian Stationary Hospital that I had joined before leaving Canada. Along with two other units, No. 1 Canadian Stationary Hospital and No. 5 Canadian Stationary (Queen's University, Kingston, Ontario unit), we were being sent to the near east and the Dardanelles. We were to have two weeks in England to get our equipment ready. Our woolens were to be stored. Later this proved anything but a wise idea. White buckskin shoes were to be purchased, as well as riding habits, and umbrellas lined with green to protect us from the intense sun that was promised us. Later, helmets were to be added when we reached our destination. It was a busy two weeks. Active duty service had proved such a grim teacher, that even the order to go East did not carry the thrill that it might have a few months earlier. In the end it would be all the same. Men with wounded bodies, many broken spirits. The glamour was gone.

Looking over my wardrobe, I decided I had several personal purchases to make, among them a pair of corsets. With my purse full of the confusing florins, pence and shillings I started out to look for "Shoolbreds" department store. "Corsets please, size 24."

The clerk with the pink and white complexion gave me a bewildered look. "What do you mean, Madam?" she asked.

"Corsets - an undergarment you wear around your body".

"Ah", she said producing a wide black leather belt. I tried to explain but it was no use. Either she was very stupid or I was.

"I am afraid that we have not got them." she stated.

I thought, "Isn't that silly, what in the world do they call corsets in England anyway?" Later, I related my difficulties to Sister Smith, who laughed; "You great goose, go back and ask for stays" - lifts, depots, stays, 'How very extraordinary,' to quote from Sister Taylor of No. 4 British General". I laughed as I retraced my steps in search of a pair of stays.

Early one morning in June, 1915, three units of Canadian Nursing Sisters in navy blue uniforms and scarlet lined capes sat waiting in the rotunda of the Kingsley Hotel, London. The upstairs maid, lift boys, dining room waitresses, door and hall porters had all received their tips. Now we were ready to be off. The hotel was a scene of activity, hall porters trundling steamer trunks, hold-alls and dunnage bags. Our moving orders had come. As usual, not a soul knew the route that we were taking, nor even the depot from which we were to leave, until we drew up at Charing Cross Station… and we were off. Only by watching the names of the different depots as we flashed past, and comparing them with the list posted in the coach, did we have any idea of where we were headed or the route we were taking. Once, when we had a certain destination in mind, a sudden change was made and we were "all balled up" again. As the shadows began to lengthen, we finally drew into Southampton to find the hospital ship *Asturias* lying at the wharf waiting for us. Earlier, by another route, the personnel for the different units had arrived, and had immediately been ordered aboard ship. The same orders came for the Nursing Sisters. As we mounted the gangway the song "Oh Canada", that we all loved so well, rang out from the throats of several hundred Canadian boys, as they welcomed us aboard.

The *Asturias* was the first hospital ship that I had seen at close range. Painted white from bow to stern, the ship was encircled by a wide band of green, studded with innumerable electric light bulbs. The Crosses reached from the water's edge to the very top of the ship. When we arrived it was growing dark, and we had an idea of what the ship must look like on the water at night, all brilliantly lighted, like a huge jewel set forth to sail. This travelling in a lighted ship was an entirely new experience for us. So far, as soon as night fell on land or sea everything had been kept in darkness for safety's sake. Even the private dwellings on land must adhere to this rule, but a hospital ship carrying the red cross was different. No country would stoop so low as to fire on the Red Cross. How little did we reckon with our enemy's want of honour. Germany did violate the sacred rule and deliberately fired on hospital ships, sending helpless wounded men and Nursing Sisters to the dark water's depth. Even inland hospitals were bombed.

The beauty of the exterior of the *Asturias* was upheld in the interior. The state rooms had all been removed and the whole painted white. The resulting space had been made into a hospital ward with beds hanging from the ceiling in such a manner that, however rough the sea

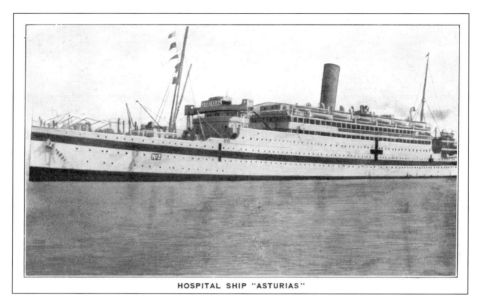

HOSPITAL SHIP "ASTURIAS"

Hospital Ship Asturias.

The Famous cake oven, No. 3 CSH. It was also used to sterilize hypo needles.

Sisters Prichard, Dolison and White.

might be outside, the beds would hang practically level. The whole was immaculately clean. Medical supplies were arranged in convenient cupboards along the outer walls. This day a group of Canadian women and men would occupy the beds. On her return trip the ship would carry wounded and sick men from Malta, Alexandria or parts nearer the field of action. We sailed down the English channel, past the Isle of Wight, and out past the Needles, the first ship carrying Canadians to have taken that route. On down into the Bay of Biscay. Till the day I die I will always remember the Bay of Biscay. A storm came up, an ordinary occurrence, we were told. The ship curtsied, then she rolled back and settled for another heave. For twelve hours she plunged and ploughed. Across the aisle from me Sister Pat crossed herself and counted her beads, while I lay and listened to the waves as they hit and splashed over the porthole windows. It never seemed to dawn on me that I should have any fear. Some hours later we welcomed the calm water as we travelled along the coast of Spain, on to the Portugal boot. We were so close to the shore line that, at times, with the aid of binoculars, we could distinguish objects moving along the mainland.

It was a disappointment to learn that we would pass through the straits of Gibraltar during the night. Some stayed up on deck with the hope that they might catch a glimpse of the famous old stronghold. We went on down the Mediterranean, and began following the African coast, on a very zig-zag course. Blue and bluer became the water each day, lower and lower dipped the stars at night, hot and hotter became the climate. Several times hospital ships passed, bound for Malta and England with their priceless load of wounded Tommies. Days came and went with little excitement. We whiled away the hours reading, playing shuffleboard, deck cricket and bridge. On Sunday, Divine service was held on the upper deck, the Presbyterian, Anglican and Methodist Padres uniting and sharing the service. We sang the old hymns, "Fight the Good Fight", "Onward Christian Soldiers", "Faith of our Fathers", with everyone joining in whether they could sing or not.

One morning I wakened to find the ship strangely still. Chug, chug, chug, came the sound of a motor boat through the porthole. "Waken up, waken up, we are somewhere." I shook Sister Smith gently. Looking out through the porthole I wondered if what I saw was real or only a dream, so beautiful was the picture that greeted my eyes. A pure white city that seemed to rise straight from the vivid blue waters of the Mediterranean - sea gulls with outspread wings swooped gracefully, dipping and diving on every side. Dozens of flotillas were leaving the wharf and coming toward the *Asturias* as she lay anchored just outside of the harbour of Valetta, Malta. Soon everyone was up and dressed. Excitement ran high, and rumours spread that we were waiting disembarkation orders... Malta was to be our future home. Before long the ship was surrounded by small boats, their occupants offering for sale fruit, and lovely Maltese lace, to the crowds hanging over the edge of the decks. Rumours are usually only rumours in the army. Out came a small motor boat, bearing a very official looking Officer, wearing the red band of the Headquarters Staff. We were consumed with curiosity, as he ascended the outer swinging ladder, knowing that in his hand he held our future fate.

After his departure, much to our disgust, the engines were once more started, and we were off for distant fields, without even having had the opportunity to set foot on the beautiful Island of Malta. Well, such was life in the army. Since we were none the wiser about what orders had been borne by the departing Major, life once more settled into the usual travelling through the blue waters of the Mediterranean. Many times we passed small forbidding islands of gray rock apparently uninhabited. All things eventually come to an end and at last we dropped anchor outside the breakwater of the City of Alexandria, Egypt. We welcomed the news that if we wished we might go ashore. How exciting it was. Along with four other nurses and two burly Padres for protection, we climbed down a swinging ladder outside of the ship, into a motor boat piloted by a dusky Egyptian, with his long dirty white garb, girded in at the waist with a scarlet sash. On his head he wore a scarlet tarboosh, his feet were bare, but he spoke perfect English. The water was infested with launches and flotillas, either waiting or pushing off with Nursing Sisters, Officers and men. From some of the smaller and flat boats, small boys were diving for pennies tossed into the water by those watching from the upper deck. They never failed to get their prize. They were wonderful swimmers, and their lithe brown bodies circled and curved through the water like water nymphs.

The wharf was a busy spot, all noise and confusion, with natives slinking around in all directions, dirt, flies, and Oh! what heat! The rays of the sun seemed to penetrate to the very marrow of one's bones as we walked along. We understood why, as we learned later, that, in this eastern country from 10 a.m. until 4 a.m., everything is at a standstill. It is advisable to stay indoors. Suddenly, seemingly from nowhere three small brown boys dropped at our feet and were off on a cartwheel stunt. Like lightning they spun down the hot street pavement and back, then held out their hands, crying "Baksheesh?" I foolishly asked "What do they want?"

"Why, piastres, Egyptian coins of course." As the Padres tossed them several pennies, they disappeared as quickly as they had come. Alexandria reminded me of the pictures in our old family Bible. In "The Book", all our births, marriages, and deaths were duly registered. As a special favour on a wet Sunday afternoon, my young sister and I had been allowed to turn the pages, being very careful not to disturb the flowers that were hidden between the leaves, pressed and treasured. I could almost imagine that sometime or other I might have lived in Egypt. Who knows, maybe I did, for nothing about it surprised me. Except the men. I had always pictured Egyptian men with small stubby beards but these people seemed to lack the beards. They were large men in loose gowns, or habits, of white material with usually a wide sash or belt of scarlet. Over these, many wore European coats, looking as if they might have crawled out of bed in their night clothes and slipped a coat over top.

The first street we visited might have been a street in London or Paris as far as the buildings were concerned. Over the doorway of one establishment was the name Bryan. Inside we found an Englishman; from him we purchased helmets and fly swatters that proved to be a godsend to keep off the pests that continuously buzzed around our faces. We were glad to don the helmets, and tuck our felt hats under our arms. Tawa's gift shop was an interesting place, almost like many of our antique shops back home. Many months later the Canadians learned in the Tawa shop how to bargain with these easterners in order to get a three shilling piece of pottery for little more than a sixpence. In front of some shops sat old men smoking large pipes resting in bowls of water on the ground. From these extended the long curved pipestem decorated with many coloured tassels. But ugh! Such fifth, flies and odours. It might all look very well on canvas, but at close range it was far from beautiful. I shuddered and thanked my lucky stars we had two strong Canadian Padres as guards. Yet it was interesting too. Little boys at every turn did their cartwheel stunts, and hawkers brayed their wares. Many small donkeys heavily laden, poor little beasts of burden, accompanied by their drivers, trotted along, their small heads bobbing up and down as they walked. A native with a pigskin water bag slung over his shoulder passed by. A native woman, very erect, with a pitcher standing on the top of her head, and others with trays covered with their wares, went by us, their full skirts flapping around their feet, and brass anklets tinkling with every step they took. Finally, as if the street might be putting on a pageant for the visitors, a wagon drawn by a mule drove past. In the wagon sat six women, their faces completely hidden from view, with only their black eyes showing and by the side walked, we presumed, the husband of the six. Then came a limousine, inside of which sat a dusky lady of higher rank. The black cowl that covered her head was relieved by a sheer creamy white silk veil, covering the lower part of her face. Later we learned that we had been visiting "old Alexandria".

Turning into a better street we located a restaurant where we might find something cool to drink. As we sat sipping our iced Schweppe's ale, a shiny black-faced native came toward us bowing and grinning, showing a row of very white teeth. Producing a deck of cards he proceeded to blow spots off them, and to perform several other sleight-of-hand tricks. Finally he asked for a piece of silver that he might tell our fortunes, then swallow the silver coin and retrieve it from his ear. Foolishly Sister McCullough handed him a shilling, which disappeared into the creature's mouth, while he disappeared out the door, no doubt well pleased with his successful bit of trickery.

The heat had become so intense that we were glad to seek the cool deck of our ship. During the night the *Royal Edward*, a British troop ship bound for the Dardanelles with her load of English, Irish and Scottish Tommies; and their officers, had drawn alongside the *Asturias* and dropped anchor. She lay there all the following day. Many of the ship's Officers, as well as Military came over and had afternoon tea with us. Early the following morning, with the sun shining brightly overhead she steamed out of the harbour. As she pulled away, her decks were literally packed with khaki-clad men, who sent up a cheer, "Are

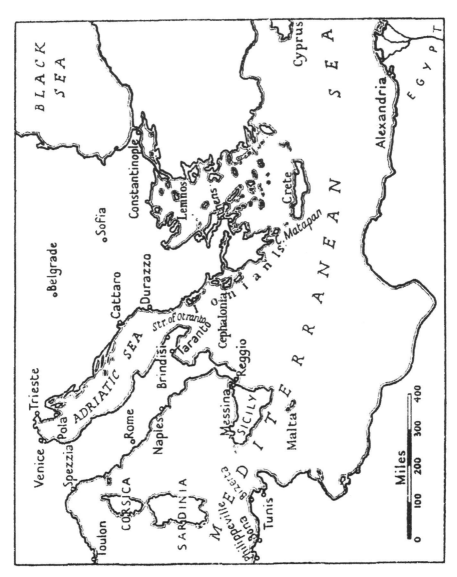

The Mediterranean

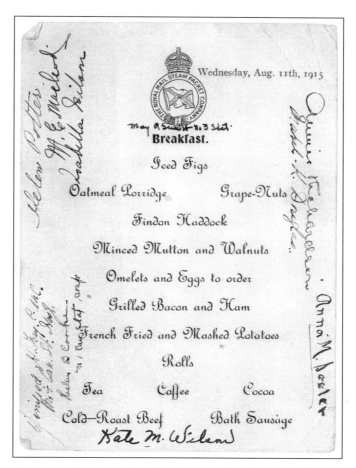

Menu from SS Asturias, Breakfast, August 11th, 1915, signed by nine of Sister Wilson's nursing comrades.

    From top left clockwise: Helen Potter (Liverpool, England; Age 28); Mary Elizabeth MacLeod (London, Ontario; Age 29); Isabella Wilson (St.Thomas, Ontario; Age 33); Mary A. Scriver (Hemmingsford, Quebec; Age 31); Mabel K. Douglas (Belfast, Ireland; Age 33); Annice Richardson (Glasgow, Scotland; Age 31); Anna M. Seeler (Sunnidale, Ontario; Age 29); Kate M. Wilson; Helen B. Cooke (Ottawa, Ontario; Age 30); Winnifred H. Fray (Pembroke, Ontario; Age 25).

we downhearted?" followed by a reply from hundreds of throats "No!". A band could be heard playing as the *Royal Edward* was lost in the distance. Five hours later she went to the bottom of the Mediterranean, sunk with all on board, by a German submarine.

The following morning the No. 5 (Queen's University, Kingston, Ontario) Canadian Stationary Hospital, disembarked bag and baggage, en route to Cairo, there to open a hospital at Mena House, close by the Giza Pyramid. No. 3 Canadian Stationary Hospital and No. 1 Canadian Stationary Hospital were then transferred to a smaller ship, the *Delta*. Leaving Alexandria we took a direct route north. Often our routes were very misleading and changed several times for safety's sake. We were bound for West Mudros, off the Island of Lemnos in the Aegean Sea, and the Dardanelles. This campaign had been the scheme of Sir Winston Churchill, then Admiral of the British Fleet. The Russians, then Allies of the British and French, were very poorly equipped with arms as well as ammunition. Turkey stepped in as Allies of the Germans, after the infiltration of German Officials for some months in Turkey. Sir Winston Churchill's plan was to use the British navy to bring her Allies relief - so the Dardanelles campaign was planned. This, as it proved, never worked out or was accomplished, and in eight months the whole campaign was abandoned.

The second day we steamed into waters literally pebbled with small islands, many of them uninhabited; treacherous looking projections of rock with apparently little, if any, plant life. We passed quite close to the Island of Crete but did not stop. About noon the third day, passing through a narrow strait, we entered the bay of West Mudros. It appeared to be dotted all over with British ships, submarines, destroyers, hospital ships, minesweepers and one four-funnel Russian ship, the *Askold*, nicknamed by the sailors the "Packet of Woodbines". There were two hundred all told to be used in the battle area. This was late June 1915. Once more we were transferred to another ship, the *Simila*, a depot ship. There we sat for a whole week within a mile of our future home. The staff of the *Simila* was brimfull of information; the name of ship, the Headquarter Staff ship, the *Agamemnon*, a large ship anchored not far from the *Simila*. (Lemnos Island was void of hotels, or other buildings where accommodation could be had. It was not even fitted out as an encampment. As a matter of fact, the *Agammnon* never did leave the harbour, but continued to direct military affairs from where she lay.) The ship H.M.S. *Prince George*, lying directly in front of us, later had the distinction of being the last ship to leave the Gallipoli Peninsula after the evacuation to bring back the rear guard. The *Aquatania*, a hospital ship, plied between England and the Dardanelles. To the right of the *Aquatania*, the transfer ship, or oversized launch, the *Joseph*, seemed to be all over the place, and constantly on the move.

The *Simila* was a very small and uninteresting ship, painted a battleship gray inside and out. The decks were narrow, the food terrible, the selection of books in the ship's library worse; in fact, the only cheering fact was that we were near our destination, if we would only have patience. Not long after our arrival, seven Canadian Medical Officers came aboard. Recently having graduated and obtained their Commissions in the army, but too late to join the Canadian Army Medical Corps, they had joined up with the Royal Army Medical Corps. They were attached to Imperial units when they arrived in England. None of these men had seen active service whatsoever, so we were swamped with questions. I had the impression that they felt very much out of the picture among all the seasoned officers, and wished they might have been with us before.

There we sat and watched the manoeuvres of our neighbors, and viewed the surroundings. From where we were anchored, directly west of Lemnos Island, not a living person could be seen, nor even a dwelling - a barren looking waste of land, with eddies of dust twisting up into space with every gust of wind. In the distance we could see mountains; in fact the whole island looked like a rolling range of mountains and hills.

Finally the day arrived when from the *Simila* deck, men could be seen climbing the hill from the wharf, and disappearing over the top. Great was our rejoicing when informed that the *Joseph* would call for us in half an hour. Greater still was the activity on board the ship to be ready. Ready we were, and glad to be loaded, bag and baggage, and be on our way. No ambulances awaited us this time, and "shanks pony" was the only available means of transportation. With a Sergeant as our leader, we started off across the stoniest piece of earth anyone could imagine. Not huge boulders, but small pesky round stones, rolled under our feet as we walked, and there was not even a goat path. For once we were thankful for our thick-soled army boots. As we toiled up the hill the hot winds swirled around us. Footsore, out of sorts, and a bit hysterical with laughing, we reached the top, and there lay the No. 3 Canadian Stationary Hospital. On the north side of a hill squatted a number of square canvas marquees, the one thousand bed army hospital. To the right stood the round bell tents of the men's quarters. On the left a row of small square canvas huts, loose sides flapping in the wind, signified the Sisters' quarters.

Hot and thirsty after our climb, Sister Smith and I went in search of some drinking water. With no sign of a well or pump in sight, we were directed to a large steel tank. There we learned that, before our arrival on the island, the Turks had poisoned most of the wells of drinking water. Only the village well escaped contamination. With the arrival of troops and hospitals it was necessary to place guards at the different locations where drinking water might be obtained. Consequently, our water supply had to be brought in from Egypt every second day, and we were each issued one quart that was to serve for drinking and cleansing purposes, for twenty-four hours. Smitty and I were each handed an earthen quart jug full of water already warm from the sun. We soon learned that no amount of coaxing or bribery could persuade the duty guard, Colonel Fox, to give us one drop more than our allotted portion- one quart for twenty-four hours.

We were only a short time on the camp ground when we heard the bugler calling us to dinner. What did the bugle say? "Officers' wives have pudding and pies, while we poor devils get skilley!"

Entering a square marquee, the mess hut, we found a long table utterly void of any sort of covering to hide the wooden surface. On either side was placed a row of gray granite mugs, a square of netting covering each mug, to keep the clouds of flies out, containers of salt at intervals down the centre of the table, and a granite plate, knife and fork, amidst which our banquet was spread. Two orderlies were in charge. One had been a reporter on a newspaper in London, Ontario, the other a jeweller in London. From large iron pots they served us steaming hot stew (McConachies). With this we had pale gray bread, on which we spread Swiss margarine that looked like butter but tasted like lard. Unsalted or plain wax, you could take your choice. Plain boiled rice and strong black coffee with Swiss evaporated milk poured from a freshly opened can completed the full course.

Matron Jaggard sat at the head of the table; she made no excuse for the lack of table linen, or china dishes that make a table attractive. She simply asked us to remember the men in the trenches, and that we were all a part of the army, all working for a victory that would come, doing our part to the best of our abilities. She finished with the quotation "Ours not to question why, our but to do or die". Looking down at the pale gray bread and wax margarine, I wondered, "How soon?"

Our sleeping huts were equipped with four army cots, each with a net covering that hung in umbrella fashion from a hook in the ceiling to the floor. Under this cover you crawled every night, adjusted your curtain, and blew out your candle so that when the flies came on the rampage in the early morning, they could only buzz with rage outside the net.

The first day had been hot, so the night was welcomed. I crawled into bed and snuggled down under a sheet and gray army blanket. Almost immediately I was asleep, for with the morrow, our first consignment of patients was expected, all from the Gallipoli Peninsula. Around midnight I wakened, shivering from the cold of the night air. At the same time I saw Potter strike a match and light her candle, muttering all the while to herself, "Billy are you cold, or is it only me?" she asked. Off we went in search of our steamer rugs but even with these all-wool coverings we literally froze for hours. We were not long in learning that, as with the intense heat of the noonday sun, it was intensely cold at midnight. Extra blankets were issued to cope with this unexpected freak of climate. I wakened in the morning with the sound of water dripping from the sides of the hut. Looking out I could see it pouring down from above the doorway, while the sun in the east was coming over the mountain top. Thinking that a shower had fallen during the night, I hunted out my long rubber boots, but much to my surprise I discovered that it had not been raining, but so heavy was the dew that the hut covering had become soaking wet. This was the trying climate the Canadians had endured in June 1915.

Chapter Four; Editor's Notes

1) Number One, Canadian General Hospital went Overseas in 1914 and remained at Bulford on the Salisbury Plain until May 1915. The Hospital went to Etaples, France in May 1915 and remained there until July 1918, when it was moved to Trouville, where it remained until March 1919.

2) Number Three Canadian General Hospital (McGill) went Overseas in 1915. The Hospital was sent to Camiers in June 1915 and was moved to Boulogne in January 1916. It remained at Boulogne until May 1919.

3) Number One Canadian Stationary Hospital went to Le Havre, France in February 1915, then to Wimereux until July 1915 when it was sent to the Aegean. It was located at Lemnos from August 1915 to January 1916. It was stationed at Alexandria, Egypt in February 1916, then moved to Salonica (Thessaloniki, Greece) from March 1916 to September 1917. No. 1 CSH returned to Hastings, England in September 1917 and became No.13 CGH.

4) Number Three Canadian Stationary Hospital arrived in Shorncliffe, England in May 1915 and was sent to Mudros in the Aegean in August 1915. It remained there until February 1916, when it was removed to Alexandria, Egypt. In April 1916 No.3 CSH went to Boulogne, France. In November 1916 it was moved to Doullens, then to Rouen (August 1918), to Malassisie (October 1918) and finished the war in Shorncliffe.

5) Number Five Canadian Stationary Hospital (Queen's) arrived at Shorncliffe, England in May 1915, was sent to Cairo, Egypt in August 1915. It was reformed as No.7 CGH and sent to Etaples, France where it remained until 1919.

6) The Hospital Ship, Asturias (12,002 tons) was attacked by a submarine and forced to beach on September 21st, 1917. Thirty-five lives were lost.

7) Sister Guerin (Kate "Pat" Guerin) was born in Limerick, Ireland May 25th, 1885.

8) Sister McCulloch (Georgianna Beach McCulloch) was born in Ottawa, July 9th, 1887.

9) The Troopship, Royal Edward (11,117 tons), was sunk by a submarine en route to Gallipoli on August 13th, 1915. More than 900 soldiers and sailors lost their lives.

10) The Simla (5,884 tons) was sunk by a submarine near Gozo Island on April 2nd, 1916. Ten lives were lost.

11) Matron Jessie B. Jaggard (nee Brown) was born in Kings County, Nova Scotia, May 28th, 1893. She married Herbert Jaggard and lived in Elmira, New York when she enlisted in the CAMC. She died of dysentery at Portianos on September 25th, 1915 and is buried in Portianos Military Cemetery, Lemnos, Plot V, Row D, Grave 177.

12) Sister Potter (Helen Potter) was born in Liverpool, England September 22nd, 1887.

Chapter Five

First Ward Duty on Lemnos Island

With the heat of the first few days came a great thirst. Not realizing how quickly a quart of water can disappear, I drained my jug bone dry in the morning. My face and hands were still to be washed and my teeth needed brushing. And I needed a drink of water, as I never had before. On the opposite cot Sister Smith sat holding her precious jug. "What had I better do, drink this or wash my face?", she asked. Remembering that there would be hot coffee for breakfast, and that our jugs would be filled at 10 a.m. we decided to share the contents of her small supply. Soaking our washcloths, we had enough to wash the sleep out of our eyes. We decided that we had better do a better job of budgeting our water supply in the future.

It was a sorry looking hospital ward I entered that morning. The marquee had been pitched on the first slope of quite a steep hill. There was no covering, as yet, to protect our feet from the many small stones that covered the whole place. As I went from cot to cot where most of the patients were suffering from amoebic dysentery or malarial fever, I rolled the larger stones under the beds with my feet. Since water was such a problem, only hands and faces could be washed, once a day. Millions of flies infested the place. With forty-eight patients, it was almost impossible to keep the pests from the sickest of them, and they were all sick. Mosquito netting was pressed into use until the supply ran out, and it took one to two weeks to bring a new supply from Egypt.

At the end of the ward a space was curtained off with a gray flannel blanket tacked onto a frame. It was a service kitchen and record room combined, for the Nursing Sister in charge. This served very well until one morning while I sat doing my history charts for the day, I noticed body lice crawling around on my partition. That gave me a shock and a very squeamish feeling all over. The partition was quickly pulled down and replaced by a white sheet. This was one problem we had to battle on Lemnos Island that we had never had to contend with in

France. Possibly the unsanitary condition of the island was partly responsible for the foul condition of the mud in the trenches on the Gallipoli Peninsula, as one might very well expect.

My first thought ran to diets. I made the discovery that I had nothing with which to heat anything. When I sent the orderly in quest of an oil stove we were told that the supply had been delayed, and we learned later that the ship carrying supplies to Lemnos Island had been sunk in the Mediterranean by a German submarine. It was not definite how soon another ship might arrive. In the meantime hypodermic doses of emetine were to be administered every four hours to many of the patients, and that necessitated the sterilizing of hypo needles for the syringes. There was nothing for it but to build bonfires outside. With a true pioneer initiative the orderlies set to work improvising stoves, and an orderly was placed on fire-duty to see that no stray sparks were blown around. That would have proved disastrous in a canvas hospital. Here, using an army dixie (a cast iron pot twelve by ten inches long, with a fitted top), we concocted our first nourishments, mostly scalded Swiss milk (canned) for our dysentery patients. Also in the same dixies, cleaned with the cleanest sand the orderlies could find, we sterilized our hypo needles for the day. The orderly on duty at my outdoor stove declared I was wasting fuel and his valuable time. He was sure that by placing the dixie and its contents within the rays of the hot sun just anywhere on the camp ground, it would boil within a few minutes. That poor orderly, how he must have baked! With all our background training this seemed a hopeless procedure, but it seemed to work in every case. I was amused to look across at my next door neighbour and her orderly struggling with a smoking bonfire. It was impossible to forget all the conveniences and comforts of No. 4 British General, or No. 1 Canadian General Hospital back in France. We were not discouraged, we had faith in the pioneering spirit of our own No. 3 Canadian Stationary Hospital on Lemnos Island, away down in the Aegean Sea. At any rate, this was real soldiering.

One morning an English Tommy fully armed, presented himself at my marquee door, with a half dozen of the blackest, dirtiest and most unkempt men I had ever seen. Informed that they were Turkish prisoners from the Internment Camp, sent over to gather up the stones, we welcomed them almost as our guests. As they worked I must admit that

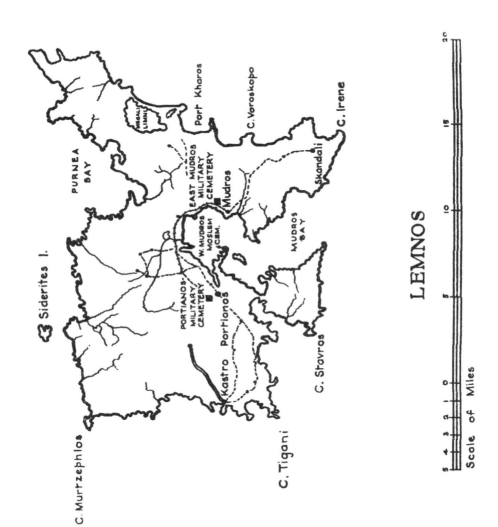

LEMNOS

Scale of Miles

I kept one eye on my work, and the other on the Turks, lest from some hidden hand, a dirk might fly in my direction. Pat, a big red-headed Irishman who occupied a bed at one end of the tent, had been very ill with a dangerously high temperature. At the sight of the prisoners he became very excited, and before I could get to him, he reached down, picked up a stone and, more quickly and more accurate than any Turk might have been, he aimed for the shins of a big black-whiskered fellow. "Pat, whatever are you doing?" I asked, anxious about his fever. "Sure, the devil is wearing British army boots," was the only apology he offered. Pat belonged to the Irish Fusiliers Regiment.

The gathering of the stones was the first step in the real improvement of the wards and campground. What a relief to have the pesky rolling annoyance removed from under our feet and canvas tarpaulins laid down under foot.

Things were not going too well in the cook house. Corporal Bentley, with little equipment to work with, was having troubles of his own, and the bread he produced was really rather awful. Padre Frost, coming from the cook house one morning, wore an impish grin.

"Well it's warm in more ways than one over there. Corporal Bentley declares he can't be a Christian, and bake bread at the same time with the stoves he has to work with." Shortly after this conversation there seemed to be considerable activity around that corner of the camp. The Corporal, with his staff and, usually, the Padre, seemed to have forsaken army life and gone into the masonry business, for certainly something was being erected. One private declared that the Corporal was building a monument to himself, in memory of his first days on Lemnos Island. However, the structure, a mixture of stones and clay, grew and grew. Finally, one day, the Padre and the Corporal viewed with satisfaction the result of their handiwork, a quaint, if crude, Dutch Oven. The personnel might well laugh and dub the Corporal the "Mound builder". He had solved his troubles. The day had arrived when he could once more settle down to being a peace loving Christian. In fact, the Padre and he were extremely proud of their efforts.

It was not too long until No. 3 had taken on an orderly appearance. The stones had been removed from the camp grounds, whitewashed, and worked into low walls on either side of the many pathways. In fact, there were so many pathways with stone borders that it took several landscape artists to complete the work. Not to mention the men who were set to whitewash rows of stones, as a punishment for some minor offense.

I was having troubles of my own with one of the best orderlies I had ever worked with. Back home he had been a comedian with a "Stock Entertaining Company", and perhaps he did find it hard to settle down to steady day-in, day-out work. But get drunk he would, which meant three days in the Guardhouse for Jerry and a fresh orderly for me. Always he came back apologizing, confessing all, and promising never to fall from grace again. Once, when he had been off longer than usual, I was getting pretty tired of his performance, and decided to ask the Sergeant to send me a steadier man. When, as usual, he came to confess his shortcomings, I decided that I would have the first word this time.

I turned on him, "Well, what this time?".

He looked rather taken aback, and then with a twinkle in his eye replied, "Nothing Sister, only I was over at the Greek Village, drank too much wine, and brought a donkey home and tied it to the leg of one of the tables in the Officers' Mess." What could I do but laugh?

With the trying climate, the dust, dirt and flies, there were days that were almost unbearable. Many a time a good laugh saved the day. Thank goodness we were all young, earnest, unafraid, taking things in our stride as they came along, facing difficulties when we met them. We also had a very fine staff of Officers to work with, including our Padres of all denominations, who did everything in their power to keep our morale on a high level. They took care of recreational activities, both athletic and devotional, in the large marquee that served as a reading room, games room, concert hall and where, on the Sabbath, both Protestant and Roman Catholics held Divine Service. At 6 a.m. Mass was held, and at 9 a.m. the Protestants united in one large congregation, with a capacity audience. Often the men had to sit on the ground to crowd in. I often felt nearer to God under that canvas tent than I ever had in the most beautiful of buildings back home. It may have been the great need that filled my heart at times for strength and wisdom to carry on.

There were times when we had many a laugh. Shortly after the

Recreation marquee was ready, the Padres made their rounds, request-
ed that all who were able should attend Divine Service. As it happened,
several days before this we had been issued with a supply of new pyjamas for the men, a gift from an Australian Red Cross Society. The pyjamas had been made from the gayest of calicos and cotton prints,
checks, polka dots, stripes, and even flowers. Every colour could be
found there in gala array. Since it was much too hot to wear the hospital blue flannel robe, we sent the men off to church in their pyjama suits
only. Paddy, my red-headed Irish boy from the Irish Fusiliers
Regiment, really looked stunning in his bright suit of pink, with loud
white stars scattered all over it, and his face covered with lovely brown
freckles - he loved it too. Padre Frost rose from his seat behind the
improvised pulpit, took a look over his congregation of gaily-coloured
boys and burst out laughing. "Boys, I guess that we had better sing,"
tactfully suggested the chuckling Padre.

The staff had adjusted itself to regular routine, day-in and day-out
work. Only medical cases were admitted, the wounded sent on to Malta
or England, where they would have a better chance of recovering, and
less danger of infection from unsanitary conditions. The Nursing
Sisters were struggling along, working with what supplies we had. The
scarcity of water was our greatest problem, as cases of typhoid as well
as amoebic dysentery were coming in in large numbers. During my
nursing training I never would have believed that a typhoid patient
could recover without the prescribed four-hour sponge bath. Yet here
were typhoid cases and no water. Later we marvelled at how few deaths
we had among these cases.

No. 3 Canadian Stationary was much too efficient to labour for long
under such conditions as we met with in the beginning. Soon a network
of water pipes was laid.

Egyptian labourers were brought in to do the digging, and a supply
of uncontaminated water was assured. In the meantime West Mudros
was taking on a very different appearance. There was a three thousand
bed Australian hospital, as well as several hospitals from England.
Opposite them was No. 1 Canadian Stationary Hospital, and, beside
No. 1 Hospital stood No. 27 British General, another three thousand
bed hospital.

Lemnos Island had been made the base for the Australian and New

Zealand Army Corps, known as the Anzacs. Consequently, new troops and new camps were appearing overnight. As well, the Colonial troops, the English Essex and Kent, The King's Own Scottish Borders and the Irish Fusiliers Regiments were camped across the lagoon from our hospital. And there was one very small regiment from Newfoundland, that always seemed to me like a small flock of stray sheep, as there were no other soldiers from North America on the Eastern Front.

It was a day of rejoicing when a ship arrived with supplies, including round coal oil Perfection heaters and small thermos heaters for use in the service tents. In fact I had been supplied with such a very fine stove that we found it necessary to hide it under a trusty patient's bed when not in use, lest a supply Sergeant from some other ward recognize its worth and help himself. It had become quite legitimate in the minds of the ward supply sergeants to help themselves to whatever they considered a little better than what they had. In fact the orderlies on my ward, at that time a theology student and a druggist in peace time, spoke proudly of our sergeant being the best thief in camp.

On the same supply boat came a consignment of army cots. For some time many of the wards had been equipped with Egyptian beds, low wicker affairs little more than a foot off the floor. "The bright idea of a lunatic," one sister called them.

There was greater rejoicing when the bugler's call announced the arrival of mail, the first word from home in six long weeks. In the meantime I had been able to send a two word cable from Kastro: "Safe" and "Well". The camp had taken on the air of Christmas, as there was Canadian mail with letters and parcels for everyone. I sat holding my bundle, not sure whether to laugh or weep; it was not until then that I realized just how homesick I had been.

Illness in the Unit

Before the end of six weeks, owing to the hot days and cold nights, many of the unacclimatized Canadians had fallen ill, with the result that each hospital ship returning to England carried ten to twelve No. 3 Canadian Stationary Hospital personnel, including our Commanding Officer Colonel Casgrain, of Windsor, Ontario. Colonel Casgrain, a short, stocky man and a general favorite of the whole Unit, was unfortunate enough to develop an acute attack of gout. I was called to the

Matron's Office, and informed that I was to go on special duty, with the Colonel, assisted by his batman Rooney (from Cork, Ireland). I found my patient in great distress with a badly swollen and inflamed big toe. He always reverted to his native tongue when he was in pain. Even the touch of the sheet that we endeavoured to keep elevated over an improvised cradle would cause agonizing pain. With a French-Canadian Colonel and an Irish orderly who did not understand one word of the French language, and whose only offending characteristic was a keen sense of humour, I was having a very hard time being sympathetic and refraining from laughing at the same time. It was a very unfortunate combination to work with.

Our very much loved Matron Jaggard had taken ill. With little thought for herself and a keen interest in her nursing staff she carried on. So anxious would she become at night that many times she would go from hut to hut of her sleeping nurses, assuring herself that they were alright, and not suffering from want of blankets when the nights were extra cold. Lying with the picture of her seventeen-year-old son smiling down at her, one night she closed her eyes for the last time and slept. In her service uniform of blue, in a crude wooden coffin, covered with the British flag, her veil and belt lying mutely on top, and carried by boys who knew and loved her, she was laid to rest, with full military honours, in the Canadian Soldiers cemetery, outside of the village of Sarpi. Forever she will remain in the hearts of those who were privileged to serve under her, the memory of this fine, unselfish woman. ("Greater love hath no man that he lay down his life for his friends." John 15-13.) A few days earlier Sister Munro had fallen ill, and, too weak to battle with this eastern disease, she too was called to rest. A good soldier and a true friend, she will be remembered too. My roommate, Sister Smith, fell a victim, and when I saw her carried on a stretcher to a waiting ambulance my heart was filled with loneliness. Twelve out of twenty-six nurses had been invalided home, So short was the nursing staff that we were only allowed on day duty until reinforcements would arrive. We had been given male replacements, but so far no Nursing Sisters.

One hot day followed another, with never a cloud in the sky. Sometimes I wondered if it was an everlasting heat in this eastern country. Such a quaint bit of the world it was. No tilled fields or well-built homes and barns. From my tent door on the top of a hill facing the east, I could stand and view rolling mountains, one rising above the other. Directly across the lagoon and beyond, the three Greek villages - Portianos, lying at the foot of the hills, Kondi, snuggled in the very side of Mount Thermo, and Sarpi in the distance. To the right, on the very top of one hill, stood twelve windmills. They were perfectly round in shape, built of stone, and topped with brick-red tiled roofing. Each supported a huge wheel that squeaked and squawked, as it was turned by the wind; gears turned the heavy stones inside, that ground the grain. It may have been a very crude method of milling, but "the twelve apostles," as the mills were christened by the camp, made a unique picture, and a heavenly one, when in the evening they stood, twelve black silhouettes against a blazing golden western sunset. Dotted here and there were flailing floors, twelve to fifteen feet wide and three feet deep. The floors absolutely shone from years of use. Several goats were tethered on the side of the mountain, and a native might be seen following his humpbacked oxen, and handmade plough. Up the hill would toil a runner with several donkeys, saddled and ready for the use of some of our personnel. On our half day off, we seized the opportunity to go for a weekly bath in the hot springs almost at the top of the mountain. Back of all this stood Mount Thermo, the highest mountain on the Island. On its very peak stood a small Greek church that was used only once a year for a special Thanksgiving service after the crops were harvested. When we arrived, the grain had all been harvested and very little, if any, vegetation was to be found, except a fringed, anaemic looking flower. It grew in abundance, but it had neither green leaves nor perfume. One wondered what the flocks of sheep grazing on the hillside found to eat, if not this ubiquitous white flower. Perhaps the small Greek boys attending the flocks would have been able to tell us. It was all so old looking; the methods of labouring so primitive. One might imagine centuries had rolled back, it seemed so like a dream. Lemnos Island in 1915 was anything but a peaceful spot in the universe. Army camps lay at the foot of the mountains, hospitals toiled under canvas, and every day the encampments grew. Little donkeys loaded with bundles of laundry trudged along, a driver with a long stick in his hand urging them on. Everything seemed to be on the move. What would it be like in peacetime? The rolling hills would host only sheep and goats

Grave of N/S Munro.   (CHRISTIE)

Portianos Military Cemetery. (CHRISTIE)

Grave of Matron Jaggard.   (CHRISTIE)

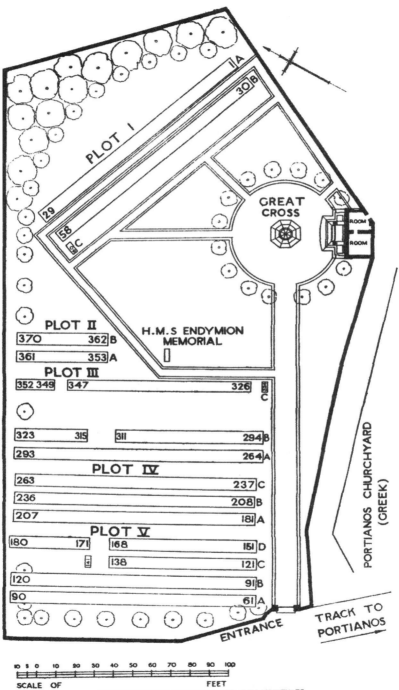

PLOT I

A
30 B

29
58
C

GREAT
CROSS

ROOM
ROOM

PLOT II
370   362 B
361   353 A

H.M.S ENDYMION
MEMORIAL

PLOT III
352 349 347   326
C

323   315   311   294 B
293   264 A

PLOT IV
263   237 C
236   208 B
207   181 A

PLOT V
180   171   168   151 D
          138   121 C
120   91 B
90   61 A

ENTRANCE

TRACK TO
PORTIANOS

PORTIANOS CHURCHYARD
(GREEK)

10 5 0   10   20   30   40   50   60   70   80   90   100

SCALE OF   FEET

PORTIANOS MILITARY CEMETERY.

contentedly grazing on whatever it was they found to eat on the hill-side, while their shepherd watched. The sleepy lagoon, and small Greek villages would nestle around the mountain. In the evenings the indigo skies, white moon and the stars that looked so large would twin-kle over it all. It must be peaceful, quiet and beautiful. Why must war mar this ancient spot of God's earth, where Paul had travelled on his mission work and people lived peacefully one with the other?

The hospital work was so different from the hospitals in France, where we rarely ever had a medical case. Here practically every man admitted was critically ill with fevers that left them eventually worn to skeletons. The lack of water, and the torment of flies, combined with the intense heat of the days, made each a hard one. Another problem was the laundry situation. Even good old-fashioned wash tubs were an unknown quantity in this strange land. Eventually, after days of search-ing by the home sister, a native Greek was located in Portianos. At one time he had been a fruit merchant in Winnipeg, Manitoba, and a handy man he proved to be. Later on he was called on to be interpreter for the whole camp. We called him 'Gregory'. One day he appeared at camp with half a dozen small donkeys. After considerable bickering and bar-gaining, he consented to do the laundry work for No. 3 Hospital. One donkey was assigned to the Sisters' quarters, where it was loaded down with soiled uniforms and aprons, until the poor little beast looked like a walking clothes basket. The clothes were taken to the Greek village, and there in a stream the native women washed them, spreading them out on the flat stones and, with a method of their own, rubbing them vigorously with a flat stick of wood. Then, without either boiling or blueing, they spread them out to dry on the ground and over small shrubs. Then they were roughly folded and returned for use. The first two or three deliveries were met with exclamations of horror, and our uniforms in reserve were worn as long as possible. Of course the day arrived when the unpressed uniforms and aprons had to be donned, and even this, in time was accepted with good grace. What worried us most was the hospital linen. The hard, crinkled condition of the sheets and pillow cases when they were returned, hurt us psychologically, much more than the unsightly uniforms.

One afternoon I walked into the Sisters' mess hut, to find twelve new arrivals, Canadian Nursing Sisters from England. They were like a breath of fresh air from the outside world. I had been lonely for Sister Smith when she was forced to return to England, so I looked the group over. In the very last chair sat a dark-haired, freckle-faced girl with the most soulful brown eyes. I thought she was beautiful. After tea I walked over and shook her hand and when she smiled my heart was won. From that day Willett and I became friends, and our friendship lasted over the years. Soon we were dubbed the Siamese twins. One afternoon we decided that we would walk over to Portianos and make some purchases. With our cameras under our arms we started off. The lagoon that looked so picturesque from our tent door proved to be a pool of stagnant water that made you feel as if it would be better to hold your breath until you were well past it. The rest of the walk was interesting. The road was hard and smooth, almost as if it had been paved by the many travelling feet. This may have been due to the fact that the clay of Lemnos Island contained a pumice stone content. As we walked along we passed the laundry man with his several donkeys, each loaded until all that was visible were their tiny front feet, and bobbing heads, as they were driven along at a trot. If one became unruly it was prodded with a pin protruding from the end of the stick that he carried. We stopped to smile down at a small boy, who was tending his sheep. In his arms was a young lamb. Willett tried to entertain him while I took the picture that I felt would be adorable. The boy was a beautiful little fellow with black curls, olive skin and shy brown eyes. Farther on, a goat with a fierce expression on its wooly face strained at his tether in a great effort to get loose to make short work of the two intruding Canadian girls. We hastened our steps in case he might succeed, for nowhere did there seem to be any place of shelter. Only a pretty fig tree, nice to look at but very little help in time of need, but no fence, nor any rock large enough to hide behind. So we hurried along, promising ourselves a different route on the way back home.

The first buildings we reached were the village school house, closed at the moment, and a large stone building, enclosed with a well built stone wall, an imposing piece of architecture for this strange country. Not far from the school was the Greek church, also with its characteristic stone wall. The door was open and we decided to visit the interior. A very stout old lady, dressed in black with a white kerchief tied over her head, greeted us with a smile. She nodded her thanks as we

Greek church at Portianos, showing our cemetery in which sleeps our beloved Matron and Sister Munro.

dropped a few coins into her hand. Handing us each a long candle, she lighted them from a taper, and motioned us to place them in a container filled with a substance that looked like sawdust. This little ceremony over, we passed into the inner rooms and found ourselves in the most peculiar church or place of worship we had yet visited. Along the front of the room was what we presumed to be the altar, very elaborate with crystal ornaments, tapers and pictures. The centre was devoid of seats but along two sides and facing the empty space in the centre were what looked like box-seats, each with a small entrance door. There were many ornaments that really did not mean anything to us, as we knew nothing of the form or custom of the Greek religion. But it was interesting and beautiful too. Our only wish was that we might have been able to converse with the kind looking attendant and ask her about it all. This of course we could not do.

Outside of the church was the cemetery. This too, was quite small. In it were several tombstones, quite like those which you might find in our own cemeteries back home. We got rather a shock when our curiosity led us to explore a very small building at the back of the church, only to find it half full of human bones. We learned later that the custom was to bury the dead in the cemetery, then, after seven years, take up the bones and place them in this crypt at the back of the church, thus leaving more space in the small burial ground.

As we passed along beside the wall leading into the village, several Greek women were seated, working with raw cotton, one of the Island's products. It was interesting to watch and note how quickly they worked, spinning thread in their primitive fashion. Several of the women were making lace on long oblong cushions, using pins to outline the pattern, then very cleverly weaving the thread in and out to make some really lovely designs. They were glad to sell us some of their finished work. Portianos is a typical Greek village. In the very centre of the village square, was the community well with two huge fig trees growing close by. Small red hens squawked and scratched and children played, all in the same small square. The houses all faced into the courtyard and, as well as having only one main entrance, had outside stairways leading to the upper rooms. The buildings were crudely built of stone and earthen mortar. Around the entire village ran a solid stone wall, eight or ten feet high, with one main entrance.

Having discovered the door leading to the one village store, we entered the cluttered room. There were tables and tables, covered with everything imaginable; candied fruit, lace made by the natives, and cheap ornaments of every description. There was everything but what we wanted.

Leaving Portianos, since the day was still young, we walked over to Kondi. Kondi is a much more picturesque village than Portianos. It is built halfway up the side of rocky, rugged, almost pyramidal Mount Thermo. Between the peak and the village stand four round windmills. Below them, half circling the mountain, is the village of Kondi, its dwellings built of stone and lying very close to each other on irregular streets running in all directions. To the left of the village and bordered by a low stone wall, was the market place. Beyond that were many smaller plots of ground, and, for protection, a high wall encircled the whole village. Kondi boasted of more vegetation and trees than most of the Greek villages. The well was just inside the main entrance gate. Here, at all times, native women in their full skirted dresses and demure white head kerchiefs, could be seen drawing water. One could well imagine it being a splendid meeting place for the gossips of the village, as they stood waiting their turn to draw buckets of water.

In Kondi, grapes, tangerines, and many types of candied fruit could be bought, so it became a favorite spot for the Canadians to meet. While Sister Willett and I were resting on a low stone wall Padre Frost came along and suggested that we go with him to call on the Greek Priest and his wife. After many twists and turns over the cobble-stoned streets, we came to the home of the Priest, a square building similar to the others of the village. In answer to our knock a tall woman dressed in gray, opened the door. On her head, as with most Greek women, was a three cornered white kerchief. She had a very lovely and intelligent face, serene and quiet. Behind her stood her husband. In very good English he invited us in, introduced us to his wife, and offered us seats. After leaving the room for a time the wife returned, carrying a small wooden tray with a single goblet of wine. The Priest took one sip, and handed it to the Padre, who, thinking the portion was so small it was intended only for him, swallowed the whole contents. Imagine his embarrassment when he discovered it was intended for all of us. It reminded me of the Indians "Pipe of Peace". The Priest, who spoke English fluently, was very interesting and entertaining, explaining the history and customs of the inhabitants, both Greek and Turk. He made a very picturesque study in his long loose black gown that hung to his ankles, and a long black beard. When asked to pose for his picture he donned a very high stove-pipe hat with a square mortar board top. His wife appeared to be very shy and could not be coaxed outside, but stood inside the low open window, a puzzled expression on her face, as if she just could not understand what these foreigners were up to.

The sun was setting when we at last turned our steps homeward. We looked back at the cone shaped mountain, with its windmills and dwellings making a black silhouette against the pure gold sky. A picture to make an artist gasp with rapture, it would also live long in our memories. As the gold turned to gray, one flash after another lit up the sky. Not flashes of lightning, but star shells over the trenches on the Gallipoli. Beneath the beauty of the night men were at war, deliberately trying to kill one another... The star shell lights in the eastern sky gave me a feeling of nausea.

Chapter Five; Editor's Notes

1) Corporal William Bentley was from London, Ontario. He served as a Cook with the No.3 CSH. He was born on July 27th, 1872.

2) Captain Henry Arthur Frost was a Wesleyan Padre in the Canadian Chaplain Services. He was a graduate of the University of Toronto, 1915. He served in the Aegean, Egypt, France and England. He returned to Canada in September 1918. Frost was born in 1883 and lived in Rosencash, Ontario.

3) Lieutenant Colonel Henry Raymond Casgrain was the Commanding officer of No.3 CSH. He was a graduate of the University of Toronto, 1883. Casgrain was invalided back to England in October 1915. He went on to command other hospitals in England and France.

4) Sister Munro (Mary Frances Elizabeth Munro) was born in Wardsville, Ontario in 1866. She died of dysentery at Lemnos on September 7th, 1915. She is buried in Portianos Military Cemetery, Plot V, Row D, Grave 176.

5) Sister Willett (Ella Edna Willett) was born in Bonaventure County, Quebec on January 21st, 1892.

Chapter Six

The Rains Come, and a Day Off Duty

It was late in September when, one afternoon, without warning, the skies darkened with clouds and the rain came down in torrents. Barrels full of it carried everything away. Slippers and bed pan basins went floating merrily away in a stream, under the rolled up sides of the marquees of the hospital "on the side of a hill". Nurses and orderlies waded around, often becoming mired as if the ground might be quicksand. I stood and looked down my ward-what a mess! My apron and uniform were splashed with mud, my feet seemed to weigh a ton. There was no way of escape. Raincoats and long rubber boots were donned; they in turn became plastered. Soon the ground was so soft that every step meant sinking four or five inches into the sticky soft earth. There was wind, rain and confusion - and lots of laughter.

After the rain someone got the bright idea of digging a drain around the camp ground, as a precaution against another onslaught. Turkish prisoners were brought in to do the digging of the ditches, four feet wide, four feet deep. Finally the whole hospital occupied a sort of miniature island. To get to our sleeping quarters or the mess hut, we must "walk the plank". Since lumber was as scarce as gold nuggets on Lemnos Island, each ward was provided with one plank, and, goat fashion, we crossed over one at a time. Sister Pat Guerin hailed from Ireland. Charming, quick witted and altogether lovable was our Sister Pat. Coming out of my ward one noonday, my plank under my arm, I spied Pat sitting on a box, a rosy spot on each cheek, and fire in her eye.

"What is wrong, are you not coming to dinner?" I asked.

"Sure when I find the blasted plank" says she.

For some reason known only to her two ward orderlies, Sister Guerin's plank had a habit of disappearing just around meal time, so we walked the plank together that day.

The rain was a blessing in disguise, for not long after this a consignment of portable wooden huts came from England for both hospital and staff. There were even sleeping quarters. We felt as if we were living on the top of the world. With the weather change came unceasing winds. There were many times when it made me feel desperate. With the wind and rain came many pneumonia cases. We cared for sick, sick men and we were thankful for the shelter of the good wooden huts. Also because of the wet weather we encountered a scarcity of bed linen and when we had to discard the white sheets permanently, I had a feeling of revolt. It seemed as if fate ruled that we were never to have complete comfort.

Word had been posted on the daily bulletin that the Nursing Sisters were each to have a full day off duty. What an event! The first full holiday since we landed on the Island. Better still, we were to be allowed off in groups of four or six. This took considerable planning. Should it be a picnic to the top of Mount Thermo, to the sunken city, or would we go to Kastro, the Capital of the Island? Our group decided on Kastro, a journey of twelve miles through the mountains by donkey, with a stop on the way up the mountain for a bath at the hot springs. There, at a small village, we could find an eating house. With the first notes of Reveille from the bugler's horn, the six of us were awake and astir and after breakfast, accompanied by Padre Frost, we started off on foot for Portianos where arrangements had been made with Gregory to have donkeys ready for the party. For one whole day we agreed to forget about the war. It was our first long trip on donkeys. Even at that early hour the village was alive with children, hens and donkeys. Each donkey was saddled with a queer looking saddle, equipped with a low back rest and a handle in front, with which to balance yourself. We could sit either sideways or astride. In either case we were at the mercy of the donkey and the runner. There was absolutely no halter or rein.

After a great deal of merriment, as one might expect, we were all in our saddles, Gregory the Greek danced attendance, seeing that our saddle straps were fastened securely, and everyone was comfortable. Then we were off like "Brown's cows," one after the other. Padre Frost led, the runner brought up the rear, chasing us along, and keeping the donkeys on the trot. When one lagged behind "Josh" prodded it with a pin in the end of the long rod, accompanied by a queer chant,"Sookey, sookey," uttered with a vengeance.

Our little party followed the main road leading up to the mountain, passing several small farms with their low stone buildings, the barns and dwellings built quite close together. We passed wide-horned, hump-backed cattle and goats galore. We also passed several vineyards.

From the very outset of the journey, my small black donkey refused to behave. It kept Josh talking and prodding most of the time, much to the amusement of the rest of the party. Approaching a sharp turn where the road curved around a protruding rock, we came face to face with an Australian regiment out on route march. The donkeys ahead (as all good donkeys should) swung off to the right, but mine did not. It took to the centre of the road, much to my embarrassment. No amount of prodding or swearing (I felt Josh must be swearing in Greek) could move it over one inch. On it trotted. On came the battalion. As we came abreast of the two leading officers, each wearing a broad, infuriating grin, they suddenly parted, and I was made to run the gauntlet, feeling a fool, and wishing my little beast had never been born. I dropped my head to the pommel of the saddle, drew my cape up over my head, and let the animal do its worst. The members of my own party rocked with mirth, the men cheered, and everyone thoroughly enjoyed my plight. Not being content with dividing a battalion of the King's army in two, the little beast, on reaching the top of the hill that led down to the hot springs, took leave of the rest of the party and started the descent at full gallop. My hat and hairpins flying in all directions, I speedily reached the bottom of the hill. My hair hung loose around my shoulders, and a great rage was in my heart, as I stood and watched the others descend the hill in orderly file, my army hat riding on the front of the Padre's saddle.

The Roman hot springs were a treat, since we were not allowed to swim in the Mudros Bay, on account of the many treacherous octopuses there.

From a long stone building with a waiting room, led a narrow passage to the baths. Long tubs were cut down into the rock three feet deep, and possibly three feet wide; through these tubs continuously ran hot water from the very heart of the mountain. Our bath finished, we all went to a tiny restaurant where we were served cheese made from goat's milk, honey with rose leaves, and bread - a menu fit for a King.

Starting out once more and leaving the main road we followed a narrow mountain pathway. On one side rose a high ledge of rock, on the

*Captain Frost and Greek Priest, Kondi, Lemnos,
July 1915.*

Portiannos, 10 mile ride on donkeys to Kastro. Sister Wilson is on the right.

other, a straight drop of many feet. Several times I closed my eyes, and trusted to luck as I seemed to have drawn the fool of the six donkeys. I had nothing to fear as the donkeys were sure-footed. It was really very beautiful, ledge after ledge of gray rock. In many places there were deep indentations, as if, at some time or other, the rock had been hot and blistered and the blisters had broken, leaving a smooth surface in round holes on the very face of the mountain - I suppose this was evidence that at some time it had been volcanic. Some of these cavities were many feet wide. Here and there black and white goats were standing or grazing on the sharp protruding ledges of rock. We wondered how they ever reached such a lofty perch. They are sure-footed and wonderful jumpers.

At one point in the trip we passed a native driving a donkey with a heavy pack. Josh shouted something in Greek at the man who drove on without turning his head. Not being content with his first salutation, he continued to hurl a volley of remarks after the departing traveller, then spoke to us in broken English, "Turk no good, finis." We hoped that Josh was telling him what we thought of the Turks, who would stoop to poisoning wells of drinking water. Bringing up the rear, as usual, when the offending Turk was passing, I saw him hesitate and half turn in my direction. Not being sure what he intended to do, I waved my cane, and used an expression I heard the orderlies use. "Emshee," I cried, not knowing what it really meant. I thought it was some sort of a chasing off order and I could not understand why the Padre burst into a hearty laugh... Later he told me that our runner, having heard what I had said to the Turk, declared, "She no lady." I never did find out what "Emshee" really means.

We were beginning to become a bit weary of the steady jogging of our mounts. Passing between two high ledges of rock we could see a valley snuggled along the shore of the vivid blue half-moon bay. Below us lay the town of Kastro. Miles of mountains lay back of the town, and just above it the ancient Byzantine Fort. Following our pathway, we rode down to the main road, and on into the town. To our happy surprise, we found stores to shop in, and, built along the water's edge, a restaurant to dine in. On a wide open verandah, overlooking the Aegean Sea, we were served a delightful fish dinner from a table covered with a white linen cover; we were once more back in civilization.

Only half of Kastro was in bounds for us, the other almost entirely Turkish, and not safe for us in 1915. First we visited the old Fort, thankfully within bounds. After what seemed like miles up a steep, curved roadway, we came to the entrance of the fort. Its two heavy steel doors stood open. On either side lay huge piles of old cannon balls, each about the size of an orange. Sometime these must have been the ammunition for the ancient gun lying in the inner enclosure. Possibly they had been in use during the war with the Persians. Passing through the doors, and, by climbing a steep stairway, we gained the top of the fort, built along the water's edge. By walking along a ledge of rock about two feet wide we could peer through the open look-outs and see the opposite shore of Greece. I burned with the desire to cross over and visit Athens, which lay not too far beyond the shoreline at this point.

From this vast height, we could look away over Kastro, and the tiny farms to the mountains, where here and there we could see a group of windmills. The very small church, where Paul preached on his way through to Rome, could also be seen, but unfortunately it was inside the Turkish quarters, and out of bounds for us. It was such an enchanting picture, so ancient it almost carried an air of awe, as if the very ground that Paul had travelled should still be sacred. The interior of the fort held our interest, though it was rather spooky. Going down a narrow stairway, cut out of the heart of the rock, we found that there were several rooms. In the outer and larger one a well was drilled down into the rock, the water at such a depth that a pebble tossed into it took several seconds to splash. We marvelled at the labour this must have involved, and how, in fact, it had ever been accomplished. The drilling of that well is itself a mystery. There were very few windows, or rather openings, as that's what they really were. It was maddening not to know the history of this well-constructed fort. Some day when peace came I would look up books of reference containing all the information I longed for.

The ride back in the cool of the evening was a very quiet one. We were all weary, and had a lot to think about, but felt well content with our day off duty. We took the main road on our return, a little farther to travel, but not quite so harrowing as the mountain path. I thought of Paul as I jogged along on my donkey. Had he, those many years ago, walked these same mountain pathways? How very far the outside world had advanced. It was easy to imagine that Lemnos Island, with its ancient methods of travel, hand-made ploughs, and crudely built dwellings, had changed little since the days of Paul. When at last we reached the hill overlooking the camp grounds and Mudros harbour we stopped our donkeys to look at the scene of beauty below. It had grown quite dark. Overhead was a sky of the darkest indigo blue; the stars and moon hung low, like great jewels in the heavens. In the distance twinkled the lights of the many army camps and hospitals. On Lemnos in 1915 the lights were not all dimmed for fear of air raids. Beyond all of this lay two hospital ships in the harbour, their green and red lights a blaze. With the many other ships in the harbour, they made a picture long to be remembered. As we started on our way again, the camps and hospitals played the bugler's Last Post until a chorus of buglers was playing in unison. The music, often sad, travelled sweet and far through the clear night air. A fitting end to a glorious day.

An Invitation to the New Zealand Camp

The Nursing Sisters' quarters was a scene of activity, for the entire staff had been invited by the officers of the New Zealand Mounted Rifle Brigade to a banquet, to be followed by a concert at Sarpi Camp at 7:30 p.m. Gun wagons drawn by teams of shining black mules, with a mounted guard of twelve sergeants to escort us to our destination, awaited us. If you have ever ridden in a springless wagon, you will have some idea just how uncomfortable they are and will sympathize with Sister Pat. For a mile or so she sat as still as the jolts would permit. Presently, no longer able to endure the ride in silence she leaned over toward us and, in a very audible stage whisper said "We all look so grand with our guard of honour, but the Lord forgive me if ever I ride to a dinner party on a gun wagon again!"

It was a delightful dinner, beautifully served in the Officers' Mess. After the many courses of wine and good food had disappeared, and speeches concluded, we were invited outside, where we found an enormous bonfire blazing at the foot of an incline. On the sides sat hundreds of New Zealand boys in their uniforms of slate gray. The Regimental band played a lively tune, as we, as guests of honour took our places in the seats provided for us and each were handed a programme. There, in the glow from the firelight, with only the deep blue sky with its golden stars for a ceiling, we listened to the following delightful concert:

(copied from the original)

New Zealand Mounted Rifle Brigade
Camp Fire Concert
Held at Sarpi Camp, Mudros
October 18, 1915
Program

Part 1

1 Selection... "Zampa" (Harold) Brigade Band.
2 Song...   Sergeant Dawn C.M.R.
3 Song...   Lieutenant Melville A.M.R.
4 Picolo, Solo...   Bandsman Sheldon
5 Song...   Sergeant Chignell A.M.R.
6 Selection "Hunting Scene...   Brigade Band

Interval

Part 2

7 Song...   Trooper Corner C.M.R.
8 Recitation... Maj. A.M. Samuel W.M.R.
9 Selection... Sergeant Maj. Keckell W.M.R.
10 Stunt Selected...   Sergeant Ryan W.M.R.
11 Selection, Romoni Gounod...   Brigade Band
12 Song, The Little Gray Home in the West...   Trp.   Jeffery W.M.R.
13 Song...   Trp. Frazer W.M.R.
14 Song...   Trp. Lillice C.M.R.
15 Selection National...   Brigade Band
16 Dance...   Maori Company

God Save the King

The whole program was very fine, but two numbers always stand out in my memory. "The Trumpeter" was sung by Lieutenant Melville, Canterbury Mounted Rifles. His rich voice was well suited to the song, with all its sweetness and pathos. When he sang "Gabriel will sound the

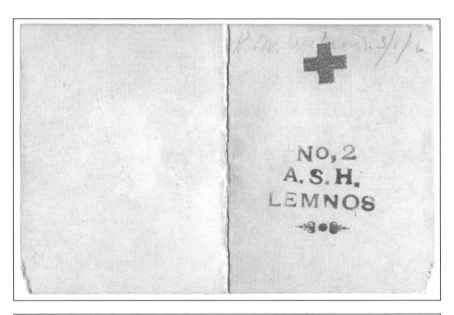

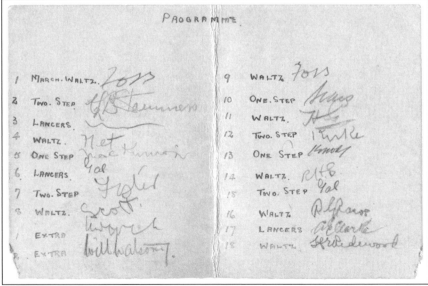

Sister Wilson's Dance card.

last rally" he paused, and away off on the hill top a bugler played the intervening measures of music. It was so effective it brought tears to our eyes. The dance of the Maoris was both exciting and interesting. One of the officers, in speaking of the Maori people, said they were all of quite a high intelligence, many of them brilliantly clever. This Company, possibly two hundred strong, had the distinction of being the only one of its kind in the British army. They were very popular with the New Zealand soldiers. They made a weird picture in their native costume, with their black faces shining in the firelight, dancing to the music of the tom-toms. They formed a half-moon circle in preparation for their dance. Starting with a mournful chant, and clapping their hands in unison, they moved their bodies until every muscle was brought into play. The chanting became louder and louder, until finally, with a "whoop," they turned and were lost in the darkness of the night. As I watched, every nerve in my own body taut, it was almost a relief to see them disappear. I believe this was their native war dance. This brought the evening to a close. After Matron Wilson, on behalf of all of us, expressed our appreciation, we were once more assisted onto the waiting gun wagons, much to Pat's disgust. It was an evening to remember. It was the first entertainment of any sort to be held on the Island, but it appeared to have set a precedent. Soon after, Colonel Green invited our camp to a lecture on Australia. He had a happy knack of describing in detail whatever he might be talking about, so he made Australia real for us, even if he brought groans from the Australian boys when he talked of the riches of his land. He spoke of finding "Gold nuggets as large as one's head." A bit improbable but it coloured his speech, so we forgave him his bit of prevarication. We thoroughly enjoyed the musical selections, and wound up by singing in unison "Waltzing Matilda".

In turn, our own Padre Frost gave a lecture on Canada in the Australian recreation marquee. Of course we all attended as if we had never heard of Canada before. We were quite proud of the musical contributions by several of our own boys, as well as a reading by Private Jones, from a new book by Robert Service, "The Tales of a Red Cross Man." Sergeant Smith sang Tolsti's "Good-bye" and, as an encore, "Michigan", a very popular song with us, but apparently new to the Anzacs. It proved to be such a hit that for days, from any corner of the different camps one could hear, sung or whistled, "That's why I wish again, that I was in Michigan, down on the farm."

The Essex and Kent, not wishing to be outdone, put on several performances in a long stone building used as a canteen and recreation hall. Often their programmes consisted of card magicians doing every possible stunt, blowing spots off cards and performing the top hat trick. Doing everything in fact, but producing a rabbit from a hind pocket. They too, sang many of the popular English war songs. One never to be forgotten solo was rendered by a Sergeant Major with a deep bass voice who sang "Roll on Restless Sea." Sister Willett said she was always seasick by the time he came to the end of his song.

One night Willett and I were sitting on the end of a seat by a small open window, enjoying the refreshments which were usually served at the end of a performance. There were large mugs of steaming hot coffee, dipped from iron dixies at the end of each seat. Buns were tossed along to each person. Willett proved a poor catcher; her bun fell and she picked it up off the dirty floor to find it was heavy as a cannon ball. When she thought that no one was looking she tossed it out the window. Imagine her embarrassment when she heard a groan of pain from outside and heard a Tommy declare, "Hit me straight in the eye, she did!"

Dinner on a Torpedo Destroyer

Entertainment was not entirely confined to the shores of Lemnos Island. One evening, at a dance given in our recreation marquee (and dances were few and far between), I was introduced to Lieutenant George Oakden, a staff Medical Officer on board H.M.S. *Prince George*. This ship later had the distinction of bringing back the rear guard from the Gallipoli Peninsula, at the time of the evacuation of the troops. She accomplished this at night without a single casualty, with the exception of a mule that lost its footing and went to a watery grave in Suvla Bay. Later, when Doctor Oakden, on behalf of the Captain of the ship, invited ten of the Nursing Sisters of No. 3 Canadian Stationary Hospital to a dinner on his ship, our Matron graciously accepted the invitation. It was indeed an honour for women were not welcomed on board any ship in the British Navy. An ancient superstition that lingered over the years, warned that having women or cats on board brought evil luck to the ship.

When the evening arrived it proved a perfect night, with a huge white moon in the indigo sky and millions of stars winking down. What more could we wish for? In the valley below, not even a donkey brayed to disturb the peace of it all. With considerable excitement we hauled out our navy blue dress uniforms, since this was really a special occasion. With great care we folded our sheerest white veils, pinned them with care at the back of our necks so that they hung in graceful folds down over our shoulders. We chatted in unison, as we rubbed and polished brass buttons, and British Lion's head belt buckles, and brushed our high black boots until they shone like ebony. Using our four by five inch mirrors we applied lipstick, and an extra dab of powder to our noses. As we threw our scarlet-lined capes over our shoulders, and pulled on our white kid gloves we wondered what we might talk about, and hoped we would not be found dull guests. Pat declared that it was a "God's blessing" they were all men, as we recalled the reserve of the English Nursing Sisters. She gave a toss of her pretty head. "I think that they were all just jealous of our pretty uniforms," she said.

She was remembering the drab gray uniforms and short scarlet capes of the Q.A.I.M.N.S., and hoped that the men would admire ours. They did! This time there were no ambulances or gun wagons. We would have to walk the mile distance to Mudros Harbour, where the *Joseph* waited at anchor. The only discordant note of the whole evening was the tracer light from the star shells playing over the dug-outs up the side of the mountain.

Very soon we were all tucked away on the little launch and chug-chugging through the black waters of Mudros Bay toward the row of battle ships, with their bows facing out in position, ready to weigh anchor at any time. These ships were Winston Churchill's great pride. As we approached the *Prince George*, we could make out even in the evening's gathering gloom, the two funnels of each ship, with the two towering masts "Fore and Mizzen", rising to a height of eighty feet or more. Half way up the foremast at the "Crow's nest" or look-out station, every hour, day and night, a sentry stood keeping watch in all directions. The huge steel holding braces of each mast were spread out, so that in the distance they resembled two gigantic fans. After a few minutes splashing through the water with the *Joseph*'s aide-wheel twirling and sending up circles of water and spray at every turn, we nosed into the side of the *Prince George*. Then it was a climb up the swinging ladder hanging outside the ship, to the upper deck. There the Captain and several Officers were waiting to welcome us on board. Stepping out onto the wide board flooring of the deck, my first impression was of the immaculate cleanliness of white walls, and sparkling brass fixtures, shining like mirrors. The highly polished woodwork gleamed, and in keeping with it all glowed the immaculate white uniforms of seven hundred Officers and men. I had the feeling that I was watching a movie, and was bemused by the dignity and peace of the scene in these war-torn days. The whole atmosphere seemed to call for low voices and quiet laughter. We were not long on board when the ship's bells summoned us to dinner in the dining room, where a long table had been spread with a white linen table cloth, and centered with a bowl of shaggy pink daisies and sprigs of gray-green fig leaves. At each place setting silver cutlery and large, stiffly-starched napkins folded to look like cornucopias completed the table arrangement. The Captain asked the blessing and proposed the toast to His Majesty King George, our Sovereign. The champagne was served in small crystal goblets. We sat down to a delicious, if unique dinner, beautifully served:

Iced Figs
Lindon Haddock
Minced mutton, and walnuts.
Cold beef-bath sausages.
French fried and mashed potatoes.
Rolls.

It was all very formal and dignified, with never an awkward pause in the general conversation, as we talked of Canada, France, England and the war on both the Western and Eastern fronts. The Captain proved a great host. After the toast to the ladies, we had coffee in the Officers' Lounge, before we were taken on a tour of the ship. As we walked, everything was explained to us, even the wooden floors laid on steel plates as a precaution in case of exploding shells or fire. The shining brass fixtures and frowning black guns, all in place and at the ready,

Sisters Mess and Quarters, No 3 CSH. Mudros. Sarpi Camp in the distance.

Nursing staff, No 3 CSH, Christmas afternoon, 1915.

Officer's Mess, No 3 CSH, West Mudros.

Mudros harbour, showing French and English Fleet.

reminded us that we were really at war. Doctor Oakden gave me permission to peer through one of these instruments of destruction and aim it. I was amazed at the silky smoothness of the turning; just a touch of the finger and the long barrel swung into position. All the while the very young gunner stood by at attention. The engine room, a man's place, looked like a large jewellery shop, with all its shining parts, regardless of the smell of coal and oil in the air. The engineers were most generous in answering the many questions that we asked of them, explaining everything to us, about how the machinery was manipulated. As I looked around, I could not help wondering what the engineers would do in case of a direct hit in action. They would not have a hope of surviving. Theirs was a hero's job. As we came up from below the ship's bells were ringing another hour, so we said our farewells, and once more wobbled down the swinging ladder. It had been a truly enjoyable evening.

The weeks were slipping along; we were becoming acclimatized, and the pesky flies were gone. In fact, there was very little, if any, sickness amongst the Staff Personnel, except for someone who, wanting a day off duty "fell sick." Indeed two Officers were overheard discussing whether they should go sick the following day or later on. They were anxious to explore the sunken city area, the other side of the Island. The cool weather was being enjoyed thoroughly by everyone, with the exception of the Egyptians we'd brought in to do the ditch digging and other labourer's work. They were finding it very hard going. Early in the morning, they could be heard coming from their quarters, usually with a leader stalking along in front. Singing a chant, he would pause while the rest of them joined in unison. We never knew whether they were singing a song, or saving their prayers. Perhaps they were calling on Allah to deliver them from any more ditch digging on Lemnos Island. If the cool wind blew through their scant clothing and chilled their bodies, their heads must have felt even more miserable. The poor Egyptians, they surely had their own troubles. At any rate they were a dirty looking lot of individuals. If a party of ten or twelve was detailed to do some work around the camp grounds in the morning, we would see them taking shelter behind a hut after an hour or two. They would, in all probability, be falling victim to pneumonia. So many were becoming ill that the Commanding Officer set up a hut for Egyptians only, with a sergeant and orderly in charge, promptly named the "Gypo Specialists". One day the Sergeant came into my ward very much disgusted with his Egyptians. Feeling sorry for several, trying to keep themselves warm in the shelter of his hut, he had provided them with an issue of blankets. Instead of wrapping the blankets around their bodies, they had wound most of them around their heads.

While the weather had cooled considerably, we never expected snow in this eastern land; in fact we had been advised before leaving England to store all of our woollens. During the night of November 27th, 1915 rain started to fall, accompanied by a piercing north wind. The Quartermaster issued British Warms or khaki great coats to all of us, and these we wore even on the ward on day duty. The small coal stove, turned up full, did not heat the place even moderately. We piled extra blankets on the patients, but still they shivered. On our way to our sleeping quarters we were surprised to find that the rain had turned to snow and sleet and the wind howled. We hauled out our steamer rugs, wore our heaviest kimonos over our pyjamas, and huddled under all the extra blankets that we could find, and still we were not comfortable. The following morning the ground was frozen hard, but the wind had abated and the sun was shining. Going on duty, we found that an order had come to evacuate all moveable patients. No. 3 Canadian Stationary Hospital was being taken over for frost-bite cases from the Gallipoli. By 5 p.m. every available bed in the camp held a frost-bitten patient. All had frozen feet, and some had frozen hands as well. The memory of those frost-bitten feet will always be with us. When they arrived they were swollen and inflamed. Only by administering doses of morphine and wrapping the feet in oiled cotton wool and protecting them from the bedding with improvised cradles, could we spare them the agony. Later, many of these cases became gangrenous, and many feet had to be amputated. It was a terrible experience for both the patients and those who had to care for them. This was one freak of climate we never would have expected on Lemnos Island.

A shipment of woollens soon arrived from England, and another problem was solved.

A diary entry reminded me of another incident that occurred during the ice storm. Padre Frost had given a black army dressing robe to both Sister Willett and myself. At the time we had wondered where he

Scenes from Lemnos, 1915. Top: No.2 Australian Hospital's mascots. Middle: Mudros - Canadian and Australian hospitals on the point. Bottom: Greek woman spinning wool.

unearthed them, but our gratitude was such that we had not asked any questions but accepted the gifts and blessed his kindness. Some years later Padre Frost told me how he had procured the robes.

So great at the time had been the demand for British Warms and woollen robes, that Sister Willet and I had found ourselves out of luck by the time we came off duty and reached the Quartermaster's stores. Sergeant Ward informed us that the supply had been exhausted. Padre Frost heard of our plight and, knowing full well there were still two woollen robes in storage, recalled Sergeant Ward's weakness for chewing tobacco (forbidden in the army). He also knew that, in a parcel from Canada, lay hidden a large can of chewing tobacco. He had kept it in his tent for weeks, against the time when he might need it for barter. Tucking the tin under his arm, he called on the Sergeant Major and did a bit of bargaining. The tobacco made the Sergeant happy. The robes did likewise for two shivering Nursing Sisters.

This ice storm was a real tragedy. Five thousand injuries were brought out of the trenches on the Gallipoli Peninsula and many men were maimed for life. It all seemed so futile as the campaign later proved to be a failure.

Chapter Six; Editor's Notes

1) 'Emshee', the word Sister Wilson used on the handler is probably 'Imshi', which means 'Go away with you,' in Arabic. This is not a polite word, especially when used by a woman.

2) Many of the village names used during the First World War have changed. For example Kastro is Mirina or Myrina, Lemnos is Limnos, Portianos is Portiano and Mudros is Moudros.

3) The New Zealand ceremonial dance witnessed by Sister Wilson is the 'Haka'. It is the War Dance of the Maori.

4) The powerful storm and blizzard that ripped through Suvla Bay in November 1915 was alleged to have killed 280 men. There were 12,000 cases of frostbite.

Chapter Seven

The Hospital is Inspected

Inspection of hospitals did not occur very often on Lemnos Island. Only once had Sir Ian Hamilton made a swift and stately walk through Ward U, my own particular pride. For days before his arrival my Australian patients had warned me exactly what sort of reception they would give him, as they had no love or respect for the man. When the day arrived, not a man let me down; standing cases were at attention, most of the bed patients feigning sleep. In less than one minute he was in one door and out the other, with never a glance at the sick or wounded. The men were all remembering the "Landing at Suvla Bay", when he had ordered the men to land in broad daylight, by lighters and tugs, initiating the largest amphibious operation in the history of warfare. The troop ships had anchored two miles offshore, the smaller boats lowered to carry men to the landing. The water had been wired just below the surface for at least two miles. The boats became tangled in the wires, and the Turks turned their guns on, causing almost ten thousand casualties. Not much wonder my men felt the way they did. Sir Ian Hamilton was recalled to England shortly after this inspection.

When Lord Kitchener was to inspect the hospital, it was an entirely different matter. There was one great scramble to have everything shining and in order before we would stand on our dignity for the man we all admired. Scarcely would we let the patients move a muscle, lest they disturb the white sheet coverings we had unearthed for the occasion from the Quartermaster's stores.

We waited and waited, yet he did not come. I was looking forward to meeting this important Officer. Only when we saw Lord Kitchener and his aide-de-camp disappearing in the distance did we allow the men to relax into a more comfortable position. We realized that No. 3 Canadian Stationary Hospital would not be honoured by an inspection tour. It was with a feeling of disappointment that I watched him from my window inspecting the New Zealand troop, who looked so smart in their slate gray khaki uniforms and wide felt hats. Later in the afternoon one of the Australian Nursing Sisters, being entertained at afternoon tea in the Sisters' Mess hut, described Lord Kitchener's inspection of their hospital, No. 3 Australian General Hospital and Camp. They had one large marquee in reserve for a store room. In order to have the rest of the hospital looking perfect, they had bundled soiled linen, garbage pails, and numerous other unsightly articles into this reserve tent. Imagine one sister's embarrassment when she saw Lord Kitchener, impatiently headed for the storage and junk tent. Pulling back the flap of the doorway, he took a good look around. Only Australians could laugh that off.

It was not many days after Lord Kitchener's inspection, when I was wakened at night by the "Coo'ee" call of some Australians. Since it was long past Last Post and Lights Out, we wondered just what they were doing. As they passed by, we could hear them talking. At intervals all night long we were disturbed by groups of soldiers going to both the New Zealand and Australian camps. Not a battalion on the march - just small groups. We were all very curious, feeling that something out of the ordinary was taking place; more curious when, at day-break, we saw many men passing to the Anzac base. On the way to breakfast we were greeted by an excited pair of orderlies, and informed that the war was over. For one minute my heart must have stood still. In that minute I had my trunk packed, including all the souvenirs I had collected over the months, and I was landing on Canadian soil.

Alas, rumours are usually only rumours in any army. We never knew what was happening or where we were going from one day to another. As the boys said, only the Assistant Deputy of Medical Services (A.D.M.S.) and the Lord knew, and sometimes not even the Lord knew. No such luck that the war was over for any of us. During the morning several of my old patients visited the ward, and told us about the evacuation of the Peninsula. Orders had come to them that things were folding up and they were to be evacuated. For nights, under cover of darkness, the troops had been silently leaving the dug-outs, while by day the reliefs took place as usual to deceive the Turks. Guns had been set so that, automatically, they were still firing away at night, while, with their feet wrapped in pieces of flannel blanket, the men were stealing quietly out and embarking in the small boats that had brought them to Lemnos Island. So cleverly was the evacuation carried out that both men and supplies were taken off safely. H.M.S. *Prince George* had the honour of bringing the rear guard off without a single casualty, other than a mule, falling off a gangplank and breaking its leg. It was then for us a case of evacuating our patients and saying farewell to Lemnos Island forever. Preparations for evacuation started December 19th, 1915, and were completed January 9th, 1916.

It was Christmas Eve. Back home the evergreen tree would be standing in the place of honour in the living room. I sat on the top step of our sleeping quarters, looking up into the clear sky. Two hours earlier I had heard the buglers from the surrounding hospitals and camps sounding Last Post. It had become the custom with them to take up the bars of music at various stages, until they were all playing in unison. I should have been sleeping, but sleep would not come. I had an honest-to-goodness dose of nostalgia. Wrapping myself in a blanket I went outside, and sat pondering the events of the past year, and the many changes in my life. Everything was peaceful and quiet, not even a 'hee-haw' bray from a donkey in the valley to disturb the stillness. I pictured in my mind the three Shepherds. I could almost see them wending their way up the hillsides on their small animals. Suddenly I listened... From Sarpi Camp across the lagoon rose the sweetest music... "While Shepherds Watched their Flocks by Night." Over to the right the Australian band took up the music, then still another band. How perfectly heavenly it was, and so in keeping with my own thoughts. As they started to play "Hark the Herald Angels Sing," I realized that it was midnight; a new Christmas Day was born. What would it mean to thousands of soldier boys, - loneliness, heartache, and possibly death to man. Death on a wonderful morning such as this? Yes, this is war... war was no respecter of persons or religion, or any other thing that was sacred.

I wakened as the first pink rays of the sun came over the mountain top. A pinkish gray fog lay over the lagoon and Sarpi Camp. Peeking up through the mist could be seen the tips of the white bell tents, and the buglers' horns could be heard from camp to camp in Reveille, calling us all to a new day. Over the mountains a plane appeared, the first that we had seen since coming to the Island. It dropped a "Christmas stocking" containing a bomb from Germany, but it landed in the sea and we never saw another plane while we were on the Island. The day was made as much like Christmas as possible, considering what we had

Scenes from Lemnos, 1915. Top: Kondi. Tommies buying fresh fruit. Sisters Best and Wilson with the children. Middle: Indian supply wagons (mules) with mail for camps and hospitals. Bottom: Mount Thermo. Officers and Sisters on the peak.

to work with. Each patient received a pair of new socks filled with smokes and candied fruit and nuts. During the morning, service was held in the recreation marquee, converted into a Chapel. These services had become very dear to all of us. I often wondered why, back home, church service never seemed to mean much to me, why I never seemed to get close to my faith, or why I left the service with no feeling of having been comforted. Was it because war had a binding effect, or was it the close companionship? Or was it the kindness and unselfishness we saw at every turn during our day's work, the lack of criticism that left one's heart free to accept what was given us at Divine Service? After the service a group of our best singers went from ward to ward singing old favorites by request, while the Padre held a very short service. The arrival of mail for the unit and patients as well, letters and parcels for almost all of us, provided the grande finale.

Sister Willett and I, sitting outside our hut reading our mail, were disturbed by the arrival of an English Tommy on horseback. He stopped and looked around him. Sister Willett enquired if there was someone he was looking for.

He took another look at her, "No, I am looking for a lady."

With a straight face Willett replied "Sorry, wrong station. This is the Nurses' sleeping quarters."

He gave her another blank look.

"Really..." We did finally offer to deliver the letter to the Canadian Sister for whom it was intended.

After the Christmas holiday the patients were all evacuated to Alexandria, Malta and England. With the thinning of the wards we had more leisure time. The day arrived when the last of the patients were gone and we decided to celebrate with a farewell dance, inviting the Sisters and Officers from the various hospitals. We had a merry time preparing for the occasion. Three huts were cleared, one for the reception hut, one for the dancing and one for the buffet lunch to be served. Red and green Christmas paper, and plenty of scarlet flannel blankets were used in an effort to make everything festively attractive. Red candles in wooden holders were produced from somewhere to decorate the tables. A small orchestra consisting of a hand organ, a cornet and a violin completed the arrangements. Everyone, even the Camp Commandant and his aide-de-camp attended. The place was packed and we danced like sardines in a tin, but we had a wonderful party.

The following morning Willett and I were called to the Matron's office, where we were informed that the three of us were invited to the Camp Commandant's Mess Hut for afternoon tea. I cannot say that we were thrilled, but rather amused, remembering the Colonel with his red face and decidedly large nose. Of course we could not refuse.

When we arrived at the mess hut, he was waiting for us before a fire, burning brightly in the fire place. It lost none of its cheerfulness even after we were informed that the Colonel's batman had helped himself to several grave markers to build the fire. We were nicely seated when two Officers, General McGregor and Colonel Angus, came in from Headquarters' Staff of the ship *Agamemnon*. For an hour we chatted about the Island, the evacuation, and other topics, including our dance the night before. Sister Willett and I did not know until we were on our walk homeward what a bad few moments we had innocently given the Matron. We learned that dancing in time of war is against British Army rules. Well! The General was a good sport when he chided us for not having sent him a special invitation.

We Leave Lemnos Island

Active service on Lemnos Island had been a wonderful experience in many ways. We had grown to know the people from the sister colonies. At first we found it a bit hard to understand the Australians, with their breezy mannerisms, but soon learned to admire their straight forwardness, and good soldiering. The New Zealanders we had admired from the beginning, with their quiet, dignified air. Somehow they always reminded us of the Canadian boys... Now we were leaving the Island, but knew that we would meet again, possibly somewhere in France.

We travelled in ambulances down the well-beaten road from our camp to West Mudros harbour. We were all remembering our arrival. Then there was no road, not even a well-beaten pathway, only dirt and rolling stones as we trudged over the hill to our campground. It was with mixed feelings that we looked back over the hills and mountains. We knew that we were saying farewell forever to the wonderful companionship of the past few months. The very fact of the many trials and hardships we had endured together had woven a network of friendship never to be forgotten. We sat on our pile of luggage on the wharf, wearing our navy blue great coats, waiting for the *Joseph*. We could see the hospital ship, the *Delta*, that would take us away from this part of the world. As usual, our destination was unknown to us. When we were all aboard our little ship, she wended her way in and out among the battleships, submarines and mine sweepers. There was a deep blast from the British Navy, saying farewell as we passed out through the narrow strait. And once more out, and into the Mediterranean Sea.

Many of the Officers were disappointed when the Near East campaign was brought to a close. They felt that they were just beginning to get the upper hand over the enemy. Also, conditions had improved with the cooler weather. I wonder what Winston Churchill felt about the whole effort, nothing conquered, just holding fast and then giving up. He had been so brilliant as Admiral of the British Fleet, and so successful at the beginning of the war in the engineering of the "Blockade". When his quick thinking had gone into action at the crucial moment, it had meant cutting off the badly needed supplies to Germany from the outside. This Dardanelles campaign must have been a bitter let-down too. How tragic that so many lives had been sacrificed.

It was almost like coming back into civilization when we arrived at Alexandria, Egypt's harbour, and found ambulances waiting to take us to the Beau Rivage Hotel, Ramleh. Situated on the very shore of the Mediterranean Sea coast, seven miles from Alexandria, it was a beautiful place surrounded by trees, tropical shrubbery, deep lily ponds, and cool verandahs. Native servants answered to our every need. It was a wonderful place for a rest. Even the electric lights seemed a luxury after so many months of candlelight. Imagine the comfort of a real bed, with high canopy draped in full white netting, and no buglers' horns to waken us at 5 a.m. After Lemnos with its rolling mountains, sun, flies, donkeys and erratic climate, the Beau Rivage was heavenly. We entered the grounds between two high pillars topped with electric lights and a wrought iron archway of very lovely design. The unexpectedness of it all took our breath away. High hibiscus trees were in full bloom. Ornamental shrubs, roses, lily ponds, and goldfish ponds, lay in profusion under the spreading branches of the many huge trees. In gala array numerous small round tables, and rattan chairs, each with a colourful umbrella, made it look like a fairy land. The hotel was a long low building with wide open porticos, and outside, stairways leading to the upper balcony. There were latticed windows, with heavy shutters, which were closed from 10 a.m. until 4 p.m. every day to keep out the heat of the noon-day sun. This was all very inviting to twenty six war-weary Canadian Nursing Sisters. Soon after our arrival we were glad to crawl under our netting and enjoy to the fullest the heavenly soft mattresses.

The following morning, I was wakened by an uproar just below our window. Evidently an Englishman was in a towering rage over something. I listened for a few minutes, wondering why the Management did not interfere. Then curiosity got the better of me, and I crawled out of bed, grabbed my housecoat and tip-toed to the verandah. All that was to be seen there was a huge tawny, yellow cat, switching its tail from side to side, and staring straight ahead. I leaned as far out over the railing as I dared, and there was the offender, a large green and yellow parrot, telling the cat off in fine form. The bird must have had a very fine teacher, and been an apt pupil, to have acquired such a lengthy vocabulary of oaths - and in English, too.

We spent the following days visiting Alexandria to see its Mosques and catacombs. We were becoming a bit weary of this, when we discovered the Nozah gardens in the very heart of the city. In the ponds there were the largest goldfish I had ever seen. In the Zoo, two poor little Canadian raccoons panted with the heat and their captivity. At that moment all I wanted to do was to set them free. I had always loved to visit a zoo, but now for the first time I realized how cruel it really is to force any animal into a cage and make it live there, just to entertain the public.

One night we were discussing the clarity of the Egyptian nights, wondering if it might be possible to read by the moonlight. To test our theory we went out through the beer garden to the back gate, onto the shore of the Mediterranean Sea. Finding a large rock, we crawled up on top of it, and proceeded to read a letter written in ink. Suddenly from apparently nowhere, without us having heard a sound, we were surrounded by what we thought were natives, from the untidy appearance of their clothes. We sat there, petrified with fear, wondering if we were going to be carried off, as they performed a sort of dance all around us.

When we were almost ready for the worst, two British soldiers appeared on the scene and took charge of the situation. They enquired whether or not they had given us a fright, but assured us we were perfectly safe, as they were only a group of Gurkha soldier patients, from a nearby hospital, who were out for a "lark". We did not consider them very funny.

Another time, we were given orders not to leave the hotel grounds without an escort, as there had been an uprising of the natives and it was unsafe. This order came on a Saturday night. The following morning, as was our custom, we were to parade with our unit to service at Chatby camp, where No. 3 Canadian Stationary Hospital was stationed, quite close to Alexandria City. Going out through the front gate we were surprised to see a company of armed soldiers standing at attention. As we turned and walked toward Lauren Station, the Company followed us and boarded the same tram. It was when they followed us off the tram, that we realized we were going to church under armed guard. That Sunday, along with the unit, we paraded to St. Mark's Anglican church, Alexandria. During the week we learned of a Presbyterian church and a number of us asked permission to attend service there the following Sabbath. How wonderful it was to hear the pastor announce the Psalm in a decidedly Canadian accent. After service Doctor McKay came down and welcomed us with tears in his eyes. Both Doctor McKay and his wife were from Toronto, Ontario.

After the first week, having visited all the places of interest in this ancient city, we shopped, had our uniforms laundered at a real laundry, bought shoes in the American "walk-over" shoe store, and bargained for antiques at Tawa's. Even then we were all wishing for moving orders and work once more.

A Newspaper Write-up brings back Memories and Cairo

One morning as I opened the Toronto *Globe and Mail*, my eye caught a familiar looking picture - the old Shepheard Hotel, Cairo, Egypt. Beneath this was a photo of the new hotel that replaced the old one which had been burned to the ground. A compact, square, modern building, it was worlds removed from the original structure. The new one was precise, its front pillars very formal and cold. The older one was very different, with its deep terrace, palms, and plants blooming everywhere, giving an air of welcome to the guests. Nostalgic memories came tumbling, one after another, of old friends and the laughter of 1916. I could almost feel the heat of the noon-day sun yellow and scorching. Then I remembered the cool nights, when everything seemed to come to life. In the inky blue sky, the stars and moon seemed so close to earth that one might reach up and touch them. I remembered the Sharia Ibrahm Pasha, with its Hawkers continually crying, day and night, "Antikas, antikas." (Antiques possibly made in Chicago, so we were informed by one who knew.)

I could see the small boys, in red barookas and dirty white gowns running along beside us, their black faces, sloey black eyes, and gleaming white teeth, drawing our attention. "Lady!" Then off on a cartwheel stunt, half way down the block and back, landing on their feet with outstretched hands and, "Baksheesh". A penny would satisfy them. As well as the urchins and blind beggars, came camels and water pigs, looking as if they had been skinned and dried, then filled with water. Filthy natives and smells!! These were the streets of Old Cairo in 1916. Yet it was all very exciting and wonderful like a dream come true, like the Arabian nights. We were off-duty and had welcomed the prospect of a visit to Cairo. Around noon we boarded the train at Alexandria station, a very quiet spot with few people to be seen. The buildings were more modern than one might expect. We found the coaches of the train not unlike the plush or leather upholstered seats of our Canadian trains. These coaches resembled the colonist trains that carried the harvesters to the Canadian west years ago.

At the Cairo depot we were met by the Shepheard Hotel carriages drawn by a team of shiny black horses, and driven by boys in spotless white gowns, girded at the waist by a wide, red cummerbund. Red sandals and red barookas on their heads completed the costume of a typical Egyptian of the servant class.

The long, low building of the famous Shepheard Hotel was a place of beauty and dignity. It could truthfully boast that Queens and Kings and celebrities from all lands had found welcome within its walls. Wide, white marble steps led up to a terrace that looked like a small lawn prepared for a garden party. Palms, flowering shrubs in small urns, tables and hickory-backed chairs served for a dining room. The now famous note of German General Rommel's, to "reserve a table on the terrace", a table that he never got to use, describes in part what I mean. The popularity of the hotel was justifiably widespread.

Reaching the rotunda, I had the exciting sensation that I had reached a part of the story of the Arabian nights. I gazed dreamily at the lush red carpet, soft lighting, colourful low couches, magnificent drapery, and huge palm trees. Diplomats, Nursing Sisters, Officers, people from far and near, were there. The silence of the place and the atmosphere amazed me. A clap of the hands and a very silent black boy would appear immediately, almost out of nowhere. Imagine my surprise when a voice at my shoulder greeted me.

"Hello, Owen Sound." I turned to discover Captain Emerson Scott. He had come down earlier from the Imperial Hospital, where he was on staff, close by us on Lemnos Island. And of course he came from the same part of the country as I.

We visited many places of interest in and around Cairo and had one outstanding trip to Memphis, a distance of fifteen miles on camel back. You may be able to understand the excitement of twenty-six Canadian girls and two Padres, to drive out along the canal leading to the Pyramids and find, waiting for us, twenty-eight wooly camels, and camel boys, and a guide, all provided by the management of the hotel. Mohamet, the guide, looked as if he had invaded a remnant counter. He had draped several red squares around his head, and bound them with a wide band. The balance he had draped around his body and they hung like dirty window curtains to his sandaled feet. When he bowed to us, his head almost touched the ground.

"The ladies, you mount?"

We mounted alright. The beasts were ordered by the camel boys to kneel. They obeyed with such groaning and grunting as I have never heard, before or since. I put my foot gingerly in the provided stirrup, and we started to rise, and rise, and rise. With every grunt the animal made, my heart did a flip. Finally, there I was up in the air, with only the front of the saddle to grasp for security. My camel boy caught the tail of the animal, and informed me, "He going". I sent up a prayer that "He" might be safe as well, as I had a mental picture of myself being carried off across the desert on a fleeing camel. After a lot of laughing and hilarity, we were finally mounted and set off at a slow pace. Ask anyone who knows and they will tell you what I mean ... right foot, left hind foot just like a pacer horse. We were rocked this way and that. The change, once we gained the hard, paved road, was glorious. The animals were speeded up, and we were given the sensation of being rocked in a rocking chair. So we rocked our way up to the Pyramids. On the way we halted to let a company of camel-mounted Highlanders in full kilt, pass by; a sight for young Canadian eyes as they swung along in swaying rhythm.

I had been looking forward to this visit to the Pyramids. Always when I had thought of Egypt, I had wondered what they might took like; now I knew. When I came to the foot of the great Gizeh, I was disappointed, it seemed so meaningless. Yet this Pyramid had given work to thousands of men for twenty years, before it was completed. I remembered reading about it being built by Khufu, who had taken over the throne at a time when the people were being oppressed by the taxing Priesthood. Using as many as ten thousand men at a time, and doing the work at the time of year when all vegetation was at a standstill and the people half starved, Khufu fed the men and housed the families, thus bringing relief to the great stress they were enduring. It must have been a stupendous task, using man power, to bring the huge blocks of stone, first up the Nile, then, by means of rollers and levers, placing them in position, each layer of rock forming a level floor, each block fitting into the block below, to form a stairway up the north side leading to an inner chamber. I learned later that archaeologists had questioned the intended purpose of this chamber. I believe that history suggests that it was built to be used as a tomb for the Sultan. The sides of the Pyramid measure seven hundred and fifty feet, and the whole covers thirteen acres.

We turned to the Sphinx, a huge statue with a mutilated nose, neither beautiful nor inspiring. We discussed whether it was a he or a she. We never could all agree.

Because it was the thing to do we had our pictures taken on our camels at the base of the Sphinx.

It was my first camel ride, and, from the time the drago men made them kneel, while we climbed into our saddles, until the groans and grunts ended and we found ourselves up in the air, I was anything but comfortable. I could not help longing for the small safe donkeys of Lemnos Island. We started at a walk, but I felt that if we kept that up there would be nothing of me left intact. When whipped to a trot the camels provided much better travelling. We passed through many date palm groves, and the patches of grass, fed by the irrigation for which Lord Kitchener was responsible, looked very green, surrounded by the white sand. For the most part the road was of soft creamy-coloured sand, with shifting dunes on every side. It was noon when we arrived at the Api tombs. Before we visited these we had tea at the Mariett house, a ramshackle place, neither convenient nor clean. After this picnic lunch, we started off once more to visit tombs; however this time it was different, these were the tombs of the sacred bulls. At the entrance we were handed long, lighted tapers before descending the long stairway leading into the very bowels of the earth (so it seemed to us). We had been warned to stay close together, and we did, Willett and I clasping each other's hands tightly. It seemed a very spooky performance for healthy Canadian girls. There were almost four hundred yards of subterranean passages, with niches at intervals for the great granite sarcophagi of the bulls. Twenty-four of these were still in position. Cut from a single block of granite, and weighing sixty to seventy tons each, the work involved in the digging and laying of each tomb must have been a stupendous task. We were actually glad when our guide completed the inspection tour and we could see the light of day from the door above. After half an hour in the blackest darkness I had ever experienced, our flares were dying so we started our ascent. The inspection had been interesting but not beautiful, and, I found, a bit meaningless. Granted, I was very ignorant of the history of the sacred bulls, and our guide was not much help when trying to explain it to us.

We were a weary crowd when we at last reached Memphis. Sister Willett and Sister Gee agreed that we would say goodbye to our camels and take a train back to Cairo. The following morning I wakened with what I thought was a stiff neck. When I tried to get out of bed I was in agony. Since misery likes company, I was rather pleased to watch Willett lift her head from her pillow and groan. We had no idea what sort of contortions we had been going through the day before on our fifteen-mile ride to Memphis on a camel. We did know that we ached in every bone and muscle. We were waiting for dinner to be announced, when we noticed a hat rack, full of British red banded "brass hats". They looked important so we watched to see who might claim them.

Believe it or not the most important of the assembly who came through that door was none other than General Maude, on his last visit before the liberation of Mesopotamia.

The old Shepheard Hotel was built in 1841 by Sam Shepheard, an Englishman. It had three hundred and seventy rooms, including the immense dining room, reading and ballrooms. The many bedrooms were luxuriously furnished with dark wood, in a rich soft tone, and contained large canopied beds with deep draping of white net. The canopy tops were covered in rich velvet, many of them in shades of red with a deep scalloped valance around the top of each. The corridors seemed miles long and were carpeted with deep pile. The whole place, including the grounds, was beautiful and inviting, and carried with it an air of graciousness.

Cairo had a population of over a million, including a very large European community. There were many fine shops to tour. The white buildings were often very high, and the streets narrow and crowded at all hours of the day and night. There was plenty of dirt and noise, and hawkers crying their wares on the streets, but it was intensely interesting. There was one important place we did want to visit before leaving this ancient city; the little Coptic church where it is supposed Mary and Joseph rested on their flight from Egypt. The old Coptic churches are hard to find; the buildings have no domes and are hidden in out-of-the-way streets. A single cross over the doorway, or perhaps a small belfry, distinguishes them from the other buildings. Taking one of our Padres along with us, we reached the part of the city that was really ancient, and looked and smelled the part. Narrow, dirty streets, donkeys, dirty looking natives and blind men seemed to be at every turn, demanding baksheesh. Finally we came to the old Greek Orthodox quarter of the city, known as Babylon. We walked once around the Castle of the Roman Garrison in the early Christian settlement. Little remained of the landmark but two round towers and a part of the old Roman wall. A narrow sloping passage led down to a massive door that opened with an ancient key, and we entered the Coptic quarters. A few doors down the lane way we found the church, Abou-Sergh, and here, according to ancient belief, the Virgin Mary rested with the babe Jesus. As we had expected, we found the interior retained an ageless appearance. The Sanctuary was separated from the body of the church by a screen carved out of rich dark wood and inlaid with ivory, exquisitely beautiful. There was a very fine ceiling done in ancient design of gray, salmon and pink mingled with black. The vault was built of cedar wood and, near the wall on the right hand side, a narrow stairway led down to the crypt, a small room with a very tiny window. A huge bowl cut out of stone stands in the very centre of the room, the ablution font, deep and round. Even in the year 1916, we stood in awe rather than curiosity. I felt as if I only wanted to touch the stone seat on which the Mother of Jesus had sat, ages and ages ago, as if through all the years there still lingered a sacred atmosphere. Was it that the presence still lingered of Him, who was born of woman of the lowest station, in the city of Nazareth? Her Son had been the fountain of goodness. He had worked in a carpenter's shop until He was thirty. He never traveled two hundred miles from the place of His birth. He had no high-powered propaganda, nor wealth, nor influential name. He was not a graduate of any university or college. Yet His name had spread throughout the world. He was not an author or a poet, He wrote no books. The only words that He did write were inscribed in the sand and quickly disappeared. Yet more has been written about Him than about any other man. He was not a musician, yet He was the inspiration for the great Mozart, and Beethoven. He was not an architect or a builder, only a Galilean carpenter. Yet the noblest and best architecture known to man has been inspired by Him.

A sermon I had heard in a small village church in Ontario came so vividly to my mind. It seemed to fit so well with the thoughts I had while I stood in the church Abou-Sergh in the ancient city of Cairo. Had this place been the resting place of so mighty a personage, that thousands of years later a young Canadian girl could still feel His presence by just remembering? In the church proper, where the sermons were held, there were no seats. Worshippers simply squatted or stood, leaning on prayer stocks on the floor. A screen divided the women from the men. The sermons were often four hours long.

We had only a short time to visit the bazaars, before once more taking the train for Alexandria. The bazaars were a wonderful and amazing place for a bargain hunter to revel in. The crowds alone were well worth watching; rich, poor, small boys with wide copper trays balanced on their round heads, covered with trinkets to sell. British Officers,

British Tommies, Australians, and American tourists. It was really exciting. It was interesting to visit the various stalls; to watch the brass and coppersmiths at work, to see stalls of precious stones and gorgeous shawls. There were Indian and Persian curio stalls, with ornaments of every imaginable shape and size, great vases of pottery, beautifully designed in many colours; praying mats, carpets, and jewellery. There seemed to be a collection of everything under the sun. If a salesman thought that you were a good prospect, he would press you to have a cup of coffee, a thick mixture served in a small wooden goblet.

Ever since leaving Canada I had worn my father's Masonic pin on the underside of the flap of my uniform tunic. At one of the stalls, the wind turned the flap up, exposing my pin. The big, black Egyptian in charge of the stall, pointed to my pin and stated, "We brothers." As we moved along, Willett made the remark that she did not think much of my relatives.

Always, the streets of Cairo were worth visiting, they were so colourful and alive, from the small boys doing their stunts to the hawkers crying their wares in all directions, calling "Antikas", as they offered scarves, shawls, scarabs, and ornamental fly switches probably only a few days old. If you were a seasoned traveler, and acquainted with this type of salesman, you would know perfectly well that most of their... antiques" were fake and would therefore save your money for something more genuine. To a couple of Canadian girls on their first visit, everything was new, exciting and interesting. Snake charmers and men with monkeys put on their shows just any place in the street, particularly in the older part of Cairo. If you stopped for one moment they demanded baksheesh. The open air cafes nauseated us, and hurried us along, for there always seemed to be a crowd of fat Egyptians who leered at us as we passed by. Of course there was a much finer part of this old city that boasted a fine race track, a sporting club for tennis and golf, and a fine residential area.

I think what I enjoyed most was our visit to the Citadel. Its domed cupola and two slender minarets are more conspicuous than anything else in Cairo, and can be seen from almost any part of the city. We left our guide at the foot of the incline and walked up the steep hill to the Mosque. As we passed by we noticed, seated in the dust, four natives having a friendly game of cards. We entered the court by a door in the wall. In the very centre of the court stood a very ornate ablution font. In the tower to the west was a clock presented to Mohammed Ali by Louis Phillippe of France. Just at the entrance to the Mosque we were stopped, and presented with a pair of dirty looking canvas slippers, and told our feet must be covered before entering the building. We pulled these over our army boots, and went on inside. The interior was a curious combination of the ancient and the modern. The entire floor was covered with a deep green carpet, so soft that our feet sank into it at every step. The many pillars were beautiful, creamy alabaster. To the right was the tomb of Mohammed Ali, enclosed by a wrought iron railing. Over the Catafalque hung a gorgeous covering of black velvet, embroidered with an intricate design in silver. The lacquered ceiling was a work of art in colour and design. It is said that when the ceiling was completed the Sultan had the artist's eyes burned out so that he could never again design one as beautiful. The modern electric lights hung from the ceiling, and seemed out of place in this most ancient place of worship.

The Sultan Hassen Mosque, situated close to the Citadel, is quite the most beautiful in Cairo, with a huge gateway eighty feet high and fifteen long, and one hundred feet wide. Here too, in the very centre of the court yard, is the ablution font. The interior is cruciform in shape, the arms of the cross being formed by four large recesses. The arches of the recesses are magnificent, in shades of terra cotta, blues and grays. The recess toward the east contains a reading niche, built with various coloured inlaid marble. To the left a door leads to a boys' private school building of three hundred and sixty rooms. The top stone of the doorway is formed by eleven pieces of black and white marble dovetailed together. We were told by the guide that the building had, at various times, been used for a fortress, and in the outer wall can still be seen holes caused by cannon balls, fired by the French from the Citadel.

The best view of the city was from the Citadel ramparts. From that vantage there was an excellent view of the different Mosques and countless houses, the Nile River, winding like a green ribbon in the east and the distant three pyramids, standing stern and still. To the west were the city tombs, and the north view showed the village of the Martich line. Beyond this were the yellow and white sand dunes and in the far distance the village of Kafr Gamous. War or no war, we had seen Cairo, and felt enriched by this visit to the world's oldest and most famous city. Our one regret was that we found Jerusalem out of bounds for us, and for the military, so we were not able to visit it, even though we were so near. At that time a British force had been sent to the city to protect it. I have in my possession a first photo of the British entry into Jerusalem. It shows a High Priest reading the British proclamation to the people of the Holy City from the steps of the Tower of David, which was standing when Christ was in Jerusalem. An Honour guard was stretched out in front of the steps before the proclamation was read. The people were uncertain just what their deliverers would do. The proclamation advised them to continue their business, and live the life they were accustomed to, without fear of molestation from the British forces. The taking of Jerusalem, and the entry of the British forces therein, is probably the most historic event of the war in that part of the world and this photograph, like a biblical history of its significance, is unusual.

Chapter Seven; Editor's Notes

1) General Sir Ian Hamilton (1853-1947) commanded the Gallipoli Expedition from April 1915 until relieved of his command in October 1915.

2) Lord Kitchener was Britain's most famous soldier and War Minister, 1914-1916. He visited Gallipoli in November 1915 and reluctantly decided to evacuate the Peninsula. Gallipoli was in many ways Kitchener's failure. He was lost at sea on June 5th, 1916, when en route to Russia his ship struck a mine and sank.

3) In 1991 the Editor, then Historical Officer of the Commonwealth War Graves Commission, was asked to investigate certain irregularities in the grave-marking at East Mudros Military Cemetery. The old documents indicated that a certain number of crosses had been removed from the cemetery. No reason for their removal was stated. Consequently a few grave identifications could not be made. Now in 2004 the reason for the missing crosses is known. They were used as

firewood by a few British Army officers to keep their visiting Canadian nurses warm.

4) The Gallipoli Campaign lasted from April 1915 to January 1916. It pitted soldiers from Britain, India, France, New Zealand, Australia and even Newfoundland against the Turks. Allied losses were 265,000 including 46,000 dead.

5) Captain David Emerson Scott was from Spry, Ontario. He was born in 1889.

6) Sister Gee (Annie Main Gee) was born in London, Ontario on August 20th, 1877.

7) General Sir Stanley Maude (1864-1917) commanded the Mesopotamian Expedition, 1916-1917. His effective leadership led to the capture of Bagdad in March 1917. Before he could finish off the Turks he fell ill and died of cholera on November 18th, 1917. He is buried in Baghdad.

8) General Sir Edmund Allenby (1861-1936) commanded the Palestinian Campaign, 1917-1918. His forces captured Jerusalem in December 11th, 1917.

H.M. HOSPITAL SHIP "BRITANNIC."

Hospital Ship Britannic.

The Britannic (four funnels) leaving Mudros harbour, 1915.

Chapter Eight

On Our Way Home to England

It was a happy day when moving orders came for No. 3 Canadian Stationary Hospital. We were weary of hot days and brilliant nights, theatre parties, tennis and horse-back riding. We had nothing to do but enjoy ourselves, knowing that all the time the war was going on in the West where we could be of some use. We gladly bade farewell to Ramleh and the old city of Alexandria, and boarded a small Castle Line hospital ship on our way home. Our first stop was at Augusta Harbour. We drew alongside and dropped anchor by the old fort that lies close to the shore of Sicily. Here we were to wait for the ship *Britannic*, transfer to it, and go on to England. In the meantime we were given permission to go ashore if we wished, and even to take a trip to Syracuse. After the sand dunes of Egypt, seeing grass was a happy relief and it looked so very green.

Augusta is one of the oldest cities in the world, and its ancient buildings, even in 1916 looked ages old. Built mostly of gray stone it had very narrow, cobble-stoned streets. Pigeons fluttered around in all directions carrying on a guttural cooing. An open Cathedral invited our curiosity. We stepped inside to find an almost empty auditorium, its floor covered with straw, yet, hanging on the walls, the loveliest of old oil paintings. Once more we were at a disadvantage, not knowing one word of the Sicilian language, so we did miss a lot.

Coming out of the Cathedral we decided to try a restaurant to see how we would fare. The waitress, a very stout, rather pretty, dark haired woman, stood by the table, her arms akimbo.

"Coffee?" we asked. She shrugged her shoulders.

"Tea?" another shrug.

"Spaghetti?"

A broad grin was our answer. Sister Seely found what she thought was a menu card, and at random pointed to three items. The fat lady waddled off, taking the shillings we offered her, and returning with a salad made from endive and reeking with oil, a bottle of wine and a dish of spaghetti. It looked a bit unappetizing, considering that outside we had noticed long tables covered with drying spaghetti, uncovered and attended by millions of flies. We decided to return to our ship for afternoon tea.

In the spring of 1916 Augusta Harbour looked very lovely, with the old fort rising out of the blue water, and the shoreline vividly green with the foliage from the many large, ancient looking trees. A winding road led from the wharf to the top of the hill, from which the city could be seen, and it looked a beautiful old spot of the world. To the right, from the *Delta's* deck, we could distinctly see Mount Etna, the volcano, lighting up the sky at night. During the day a pinkish smoke rose high in the air. Once again we were disappointed that we were not nearer to this curiosity. We were told that a daring airman had deliberately dropped a bomb into the very heart of it, just to see what would happen... nothing did!

We were thrilled to see the big four-funnel hospital ship *Britannic* sail majestically into the harbour, making all the other ships look like rowboats beside her, and announcing her arrival with a musical boom. Knowing that we were to be transferred to her we were ready and waiting. Dressed in our navy blue, brass-studded uniforms, and scarlet lined capes whipped back by the strong breeze, we were more conspicuous than we realized. At any rate, as we left our transport boat and slowly climbed the swinging ladder up the side to the seventh deck, a British Royal Army Medical Corps Corporal, watching our ascent with interest, turned to a private beside him, and audibly remarked, "Lord, see what's coming, a brass band".

Suddenly, without warning, the private shot out his hand and hit the Corporal full in the face. Later we learned, through one of the ship's Nursing Sisters, that the private was a boy from Buffalo, New York, who had resented both the tone and remark of the English Corporal, possibly because we were all from North America. For his chivalrous act he was charged and placed in the guard house, known to our men as the Hotel de Clink. We never saw the boy from Buffalo again but, needless to say, as long as he was a prisoner for our sake, he never lacked reading matter or fresh fruit while we were on board ship.

The *Britannic*, sister ship to the *Titanic* that met such a tragic end, was by far the largest ship we had ever traveled on. Not being completed when war broke out, she was converted into a hospital ship. When

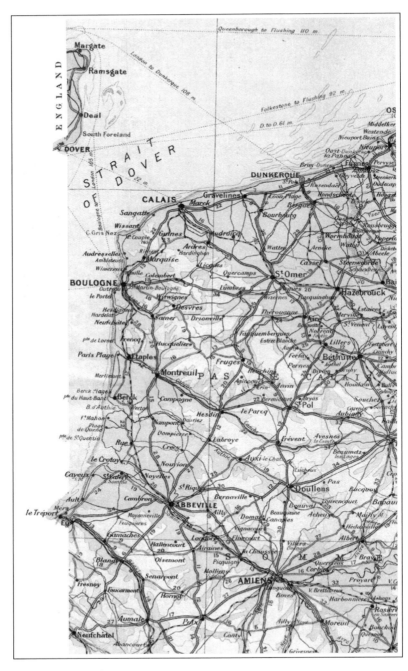

Map of the French coast.

Drawn by H. W. Koekkoek

Sinking of Anglia

we came aboard there were six thousand persons on board, including crew, medical staff, Nursing Sisters and our own unit, and almost a thousand wounded, returning to England from the Dardanelles. The Officers and Nursing Staff of No. 3 Canadian Stationary Hospital occupied the seventh level and deck. The balance of the ship was out of bounds for us, so we were never able to explore her as we would like to have done.

The trip down the Mediterranean was a rough one, as we ran into storms on both the Mediterranean and the Bay of Biscay. So high were the rolling waves that the huge ship was tossed around like a feather. The outer decks were unsafe to venture out on. Sitting on fastened-down chairs, we passed the time by playing bridge. It was a relief when we steamed into Southampton Harbour. Then we were informed that we were not to have "shore leave". The best that we could do was to stand on the upper deck, and view our surroundings, and bemoan our luck.

About 5 p.m. we were transferred to a smaller transport ship, and shortly after dark sailed out into the English Channel, once more destined for France. It was perhaps the weirdest night that any of us had experienced since leaving Canada. Soon after we left the harbour it started to rain and blow. Being once more in the land where lights were forbidden, either on or off sea, the little ship's deck was shrouded in darkness. Everything seemed to be flapping and swinging and, being a very small craft, it creaked and groaned as it was tossed about in the angry waters. Even the swish of our rubber raincoats made eerie noises as we walked about.

To make matters worse, we were informed that the hospital ship *Anglia*, which ferried between France and England, had been sunk the night before by a German submarine; also that the wharfinger at Le Havre had been arrested as a German spy. Our one comfort was that the Medical Officer on the boat was a Canadian from Portage La Prairie, Manitoba. He did everything in his power to keep our morale up, and make the crossing as comfortable as possible. When we arrived at Le Havre, we were taken to an empty detail hospital, where a merry little English sister made us welcome for the night. Early in the morning we boarded a train for Paris, where we were to remain for the night. The second day found us back again in Boulogne. To me it looked very familiar, even a bit like home, after our stay in the East.

As we stood waiting outside the Louvre Hotel, a battalion of Canadians came marching down from the wharf, taking a left turn over the bridge and climbing the long hill. A line of gray ambulances could be seen leaving the train depot close by; some for No. 2 Canadian Stationary Hospital at Outreau, others for No. 3 Canadian General Hospital (McGill University, Montreal, Que.) on the east hill, or one of the Imperial Hospitals. The place was alive with soldiers; Belgian Officers, with their trim uniforms and jaunty caps with the gold tassel swinging from the front of them; French soldiers and Officers; Scotsmen in colourful kilts; a lone Gurkha walking along looking very much out of place, with his short beard, long khaki tunic girded in at the waist, and his wrapped turban; and a group of Officers and their batmen, their faces registering disbelief at the fact that they were bound for the ferry and home. Yes, Boulogne was a busy place in the spring of 1916.

Sister Willett and I were detailed to No. 2 Canadian Stationary Hospital, until our own personnel and equipment would be ready for us. It was Sister Willett's first visit to France. Matron Strong welcomed us, and we hoped that we would not be parted in the shuffle, as so often happened. We were now such close friends that the unit called us the Siamese twins. So far we had never been separated; time off, half days off - our time was always scheduled the same.

Our stay at No. 2 Canadian Stationary was very short, and very happy. Our new home was set up on the East Hill of Boulogne, and quite close to No. 3 Canadian General Hospital. The officers and men were ready for us. Almost immediately our beds were filled with surgical cases. As well as the Marquees we had a very fine line of portable huts, including an orderly room, officers' office and a splendid operating room and postoperative ward. With the advantage of plenty of water, and a good supply of white linen, it was an easy matter to keep everything immaculately clean. The patients were constantly changing, having gone through the Casualty Clearing Station at the front line, then by train to the base hospital, where they were held until they were either declared fit to return to their regiments or transferred to England.

Sometimes we had a laughable collection. For instance, at one time, in the end bed lay a very tall English barrister, while at the other end of

The Quay at Boulogne; Taking wounded on board in France.

the hut lay a good soldier, a dray man, who all day long in his delirium drove his horse Sam. An Australian cattleman, who, when his temperature ran high, was not accountable for what he said, insisted that the English barrister had stolen a "Quid" from him. Finally I had to place a screen at the foot of the offending lawyer's bed to hide him from view.

In another bed a boy with a mop of black curls, a professional dancer, had a terrible gunshot wound in his knee. Everything possible had been done to save his leg. Finally Captain McAuley said that it must be amputated. I left the ward while Captain McAuley broke the bad news to the boy, and my heart ached. After the Officer's visit, I found Private Foster quite perked up.

"Sister, no more tubes for the old knee; rather topping, but there goes my old job."

I asked him what he had done in civilian life, and was surprised to learn that he had been end man in "Tonight's the Night" a musical comedy we had heard while we were in London, England. What a horrid trick fate had played on a boy as plucky as Private Foster.

On my last two trips to Boulogne I had seen very little of it but the Louvre Hotel and the busy wharf. Now in 1916, we had come to stay. We found it very interesting. Boulogne was a very old seaport town. From its layout and general appearance one might imagine that at one time it might have been a group of bluffs or hills, and a little town had been built up and around these hills lying on the east and west of the river, a natural dividing line. Leading east along the English Channel front, was a very fine promenade with many imposing buildings, a casino and several hotels. Several of these hotels had been taken over by the British War Office in England and converted into hospitals and military offices. However, it was easy to picture what a gay place it must have been in peacetime. In the meantime it made an excellent setting for the war wounded men. Colonel McCrae, author of "In Flanders Field", had been a patient and had died, and been buried in a military cemetery nearby at Wimereux.

The business section of Boulogne was very modern, with fine stores to shop in and numerous cafes where you could sit and enjoy a cup of coffee and enjoy a view of the English Channel. Needless to say, the place was always packed with officers, Nursing Sisters and privates, both Colonial and Imperial. As with all other buildings in France the architecture was very elaborate, the doors and windows surrounded with small, wrought iron-railed verandahs. These railings had many intricate designs, making them attractive and unique. One of the finest views of the whole town is from the old Fort that stands on the highest peak of one of the hills on the east side of the river. To reach it you must enter a wide old archway built of gray stone, built perhaps several hundred years ago. Steps lead up to the ramparts. From there is a splendid view of the whole city, the harbour with its many mastheads, and the English Channel. Over the channel at all hours could be seen the "Silver Queen", a very large Zeppelin constantly on patrol between France and England during the war. At the foot of the fort the red-tile roofed, gray stone dwellings, peeped through the green trees to add a finishing touch to a lovely picture. Quite close to the gateway at the bottom of the hill was a very dignified Roman Catholic Cathedral. To reach the residential section of the town, one could take the street car trolley, but we usually preferred to walk, as the street twisted and turned up the hill, and there were many small stores and interesting gift shops to browse in. These buildings were ancient looking, more so than those found in the business section of the town below. The residential and more fashionable homes were found at the top of the hill.

Following this road you would eventually come to No. 3 Canadian General Hospital. Beyond this was the Detail Camp, where patients were sent, having recovered from their wounds, before going back up the line and joining their regiments. Our own No. 3 Canadian Hospital lay almost beside the Detail Camp on the top of the hill overlooking the village of Wimereux and the English Channel, opposite the White Cliffs of Dover. A rambling street car line, with the world's worst service, wound in and out through the town and as far as Wimereux, two or three miles east of Boulogne. Wimereux was taken over almost completely by the British Government War Office, and the finest hotels were converted into Hospitals for sick Nursing Sisters and Officers.

In the evening, if you were unfortunate enough to travel by street car from Wimereux to Boulogne, you would find it crowded with fishermen and women who had been working all day with the fish nets, and the air would reek of the smell of fish.

The costumes of the women were unique and attractive, with wide

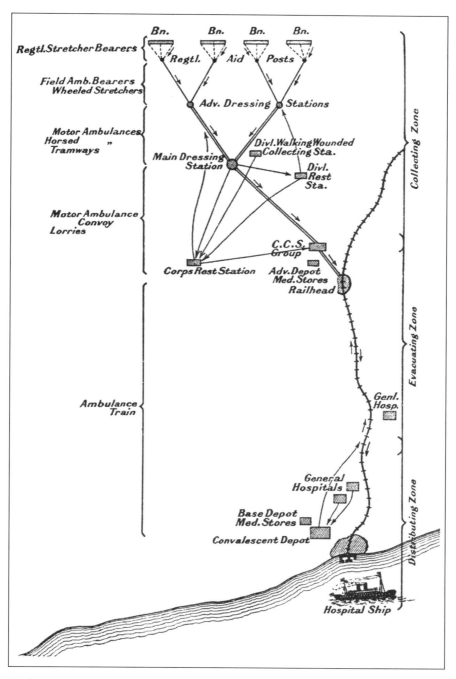

Medical arrangements in the Field.

full skirts and tight fitting bodice, usually black in colour, under short white aprons tied with a bow in the back. Over the hair was worn a white lace bonnet with a stiff, fluted, lace frill, standing up fan-like around the face.

We did like to visit the market place. All along one side stood the quaint, covered one-horse drays, the round, pudgy horses munching hay from a rack, and looking very content and peaceful. In the centre of the square were the stalls, heavy with their loads of farm produce, dressed fowl, vegetables, and fruit. Once we noticed a sign reading "Pommes Canadiennes". At that time of year we knew perfectly well that the apples had never been grown in Canada. We usually found our way to the flower stalls, to admire the banks of many coloured blooms, freezia, Shasta daisies, roses and many more. For a few francs we could buy as many flowers as our arms could hold. These we used to decorate our wards. Usually the market was a very quiet place, the only discordant sound the occasional unearthly shriek of "Poisson" from a lace fan-topped peasant selling her fish.

In 1916 the streets were always crowded with people. Khaki-clad men of the British army, and the blue-gray of the French Officers and non-commissioned Officers were always predominant. We were amused one day by one of our boys. He had gone downtown alone, saluting every man he met with a blue-gray uniform. Much to his disgust he later found that he had saluted, he felt, every Corporal in the French army.

At almost every hour of the day or night battalions of men were arriving; Englishmen, Irishmen and proud looking Scotsmen in their colourful kilts. What a thrill to see a Canadian battalion, how we scanned every face to see if there might be a familiar one. At all times the restaurants and stores were filled with the military looking for souvenirs to send back home before going back up the line to the trenches and active service. Boulogne was an exceedingly busy place in 1916.

At the end of the avenue leading from the camp gateway stood the Napoleon Monument, many feet high. By climbing the inside spiral stairway to the top and standing on a very narrow platform, one had a splendid view of the English Channel and surrounding country. The people of France were fond of telling visitors that at one time the statue of Napoleon stood facing England, but that it had gradually turned until it faced Germany. Walking along the avenue, Willett and I spotted a maple tree, and wondered if it felt like a foreigner too.

While in the East we had spent most of our off-duty time reading or writing letters. There had been so few things to do, with the exception of riding a donkey the eight miles up the mountain to the hot springs for a bath. In Boulogne the Crystal Palace had been taken over, and converted into a club house for Nursing Sisters, both Imperial and Colonial. This was well patronized, not the least of its attraction being the fact that any time of the day or evening, for a franc, we could enjoy a hot bath in a real tub. After the months of primitive living on the Island of Lemnos, France was a joy.

The days were running along smoothly, days full to the brim with hard work, all surgical cases, and many shell shock victims. Sister Pat accidentally stumbled on a cure for at least one shell shocked victim in her ward who had lost his power of speech. One morning coming on duty, looking as usual, like a pink rose, she hurried to her service table, threw back the lid of a small tin box that she used to hold her pencils and small articles and out jumped a small mouse! Pat gave an unearthly scream, and the shell-shock case followed suit. Sitting straight up in his cot, with the perspiration running down his face and shaking in every limb he cried "Sister, I can talk, I can talk!" And with that reaction he burst into tears. Little did the wag who had caught the mouse and placed it in the box realize the good deed that he had done that day. The Medical Officer later explained that it was the unexpected shock from the Sister's scream that had restored his voice.

Sister Row's men were having a heated argument involving a number of Australians and Canadians, with a sprinkling of men from the Irish Bantam regiment, over politics. As the controversy grew hotter among the Colonials, the little Irishmen threw in a suggestion. Then the fight was on in earnest, with the Canadians and Australians both against the old country men, until the Sister, coming to the rescue, suggested she bring in a referee. It seemed logical that the Colonials might argue among themselves if they wished, but one word from the Imperial and both forces joined in defense of the other. We were a cliquish family.

To Canadian No. 3 Stationary Hospital, in with a load of wounded men, came a bugler, just a little chap. We wondered how the British

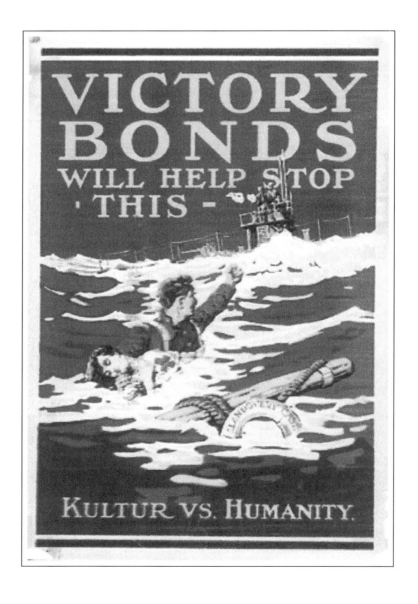

A ward, No. 7 CGH Etaples, France. (C80026)

Columbia regiment had ever been able to bring him over. At any rate Nex was there through the efforts of the Commanding Officer. Nex had been up to the front trenches and decided that he had had enough of war. He had also learned that in England there was a battalion comprised of boys who had managed, like Nex, to slip into the army while under age. If it was possible for him to get over to England, he had a brother in training in a Canadian camp who could claim him and have him attached to the Boys' battalion. That would mean remaining in England until his eighteenth birthday. He was, at the time, perhaps fifteen years of age.

Nex did not have the advantage of a wound to help him along. Some of the boys suggested that he pretend he was a shell shock case. After that Nex refused to eat or talk, although we had a suspicion he was being well fed in the Sergeants' Mess. At any time of the night Nex would make it a point to run into one of the Sisters, always looking straight ahead, a vacant expression on his face. We all knew that he was over-playing the part but it amused us to go along with Nex. When finally he was tagged for England he recovered enough to say farewell to all of us. By the time he was safely on the ferry he would be fully recovered in body and mind. (A short time ago, I read the account of the death of a veteran of the first war, in Vancouver, stating that he had joined the army when he was fifteen, as a bugler. While reading the account I felt sure that this must have been our Nex, although I had forgotten his real name entirely.)

Nex was not the only soldier weary of the war who wanted to get to England at least for a rest, and many were the ruses resorted to, to fool the Sister or Medical Officer. Quite a common and stupid one, was to ask for a hot water bottle just before the hour to take the temperatures. Knowing that we used two thermometers, it was an easy matter, while the pulse of the patient in the next bed was being taken, to remove the thermometer from one's mouth and touch the mercury end to the hot water bottle. This worked just fine, as long as the bottle had cooled off enough, but it was disastrous when the register rose to 108 or 110 degrees. Sometimes it must have been a streak of cussedness on my part that always made me remark, "Almost normal today", even when, down in my heart, I was sorry for them, especially if I knew that they had been at the front for months. I will admit there were times I really did not play fair, and made a wrong register on my chart.

One morning two big Canadian boys from Regina, Saskatchewan were admitted. They were both tagged as shell-shock cases. When the Medical Officer for the day made his rounds, Private McDermott complained of an excruciating headache. His distressed expression added validity to the description of the pain. When Captain Scott turned to Private McCarthy, McCarthy burst out laughing, then tried to blame the laughter on his nerves. For days, on every visit the Medical Officer made, the same thing happened. I was beginning to feel a bit suspicious. Finally the time came for all patients to be moved. Captain Scott went from patient to patient listing those for England and those for Detail camp; this meant back up the line. Stopping at McDermott's bed he listed him for England. Turning to McCarthy he said, "You are looking pretty fit. Feeling better?"

"Yes Sir" answered McCarthy.

"Detail camp, Sister".

When McCarthy came to say goodbye I asked him what the story had really been. He told me that the two of them had enlisted together back in Canada and gone to France together. For months they had not had home leave because something always turned up to interfere when it came along. The regiment would be moved or some other cause would forestall their leave. Apparently they led charmed lives, for no matter how often they went over "The Top", they came out without a scratch. They were becoming fed up with the whole affair, since leave seemed to be denied them. They decided to "work it," determining that shell shock was the easiest bluff to put over. They managed to get through to our Base hospital. However, when Captain Scott made McDermott's examination, McCarthy had taken one look at his friend's face and expression, and, finding that he was making such a good job of acting the part, McCarthy simply could not keep from laughing... away flew his chance for a visit to England. I felt sorry for him as I watched him shoulder his pack and march off with the others. I also wished that his sense of humour had not been so keen, as he turned and gave me a salute.

Chapter Eight; Editor's Notes

1) The Hospital Ship Britannic (48,158 tons) was the sister ship of the Titanic. She served in the Aegean, 1915-1916. The Britannic struck a mine and sank off the Greek coast on November 21st, 1916. Twenty-one lives were lost.

2) The Hospital Ship Anglia (1,862 tons) struck a mine and sank in the English Channel on November 17th, 1915. Twenty-five lives were lost.

3) Lieutenant Colonel John McCrae (1872-1918) was a graduate of the University of Toronto in Medicine, 1910. He served in the Boer War. McCrae sailed with the First Contingent in 1914 as the Medical Officer of the 1st Canadian Artillery Brigade. It was while serving with this unit during the Second Battle of Ypres he composed his famous poem,"In Flanders Fields." From June 1915 until his death from pneumonia on January 28th, 1918 he was in charge of No.3 Canadian General Hospital (McGill). He was buried with Full Military Honours in Wimereux Communal Cemetery.

4) The Column of Napoleon's Grand Army still overlooks the English Channel, not far from Terlincthun British Cemetery. The cemetery is in the little valley where Sister Wilson took her walks. Where the valley meets the coast is Fort de la Creche, part of Hitler's Atlantic Wall. The Fort was captured by the Queen's Own Rifles of Canada in September 1944.

Chapter Nine
Casualty Clearing Station Duty

Every day was proving the same as the day before; evening evacuations and admitting new patients, the worst being those with gangrene, with its sickening odour. After service in the east, with its shortage of water and clean linen, we felt as if we were living in the lap of luxury. Our mess hut even boasted a set of semi-porcelain dishes. The menu each day, under the direction of a competent Home Sister, was all that could be desired. The patients' beds were covered with white coverlets, and there was always an abundance of flowers in the wards on the bedside lockers. Red Cross Societies from the colonies were supplying the wards with almost everything we might need.

I am reminded of a supply of bed socks that came from a well wishing Australian Red Cross Society. Of dainty shades of yellow, pink, pale blue and mauve, these socks were at least three quarters of a yard long and five inches wide. The Matron, with a twinkle in her eye, handed me an armful. I wondered whatever I would use them for, then I had a brain wave. I found that, by doubling the legs of the socks up inside, I was able to convert them into toques. So away went the Australian Red Cross socks on the heads of the British Tommies, homeward bound and happy.

Often in the evening, Willett and I took a walk down the Calais road past the Napoleon monument to a place we called the happy valley, a lovely spot between two hills wooded with trees. At the base of the hills ran a tinkling little brook with a well beaten pathway alongside. A little old mill completed the picture. On an afternoon off, I was sitting reading by the stream when I noticed the grass move. Not knowing exactly what to expect, I sat and watched. Finally a gray head, two black eyes and two pointed ears appeared between the tall grass, and a small creature and I sat looking at one another. I knew it was not a muskrat, so, grasping my swagger stick very tightly, I sat very still and waited. Slowly there appeared, between the tall grasses, one of the biggest rats I have ever heard of, quite the size of a half grown kitten. I am not sure which one made the quickest move, the French rat or me.

I made a note in my mind not to laugh again when I heard the boys telling tall stories of the rats up in the trenches. I could well believe them.

With all the comforts we were enjoying, Sister Willett and I were wishing for something more than army base duty. We may even have been feeling a bit ashamed of all the luxuries we were enjoying, and tired of the sameness of the days. Even the fife and drum band of the Detail camp that passed each morning, piping the boys along to the tune of "Pretty Red Wing", back up the lines to the trenches, seemed to be getting on our nerves. We finally volunteered for Casualty Clearing Station duty. We had almost come to the conclusion that our request was being ignored when, one afternoon, the Matron came to my ward with orders for me to go off duty, and be ready to catch a train in an hour. Sister Willett and I were being sent to No. 44 British Casualty Clearing Station at Puchevillers, on the Somme, to relieve. When I reached our tent, I found Sister Willett almost ready and a couple of the other girls busy packing my hold-all. They called us lucky... It at least was what we had asked for.

It had been a particularly busy day and we were both weary, yet we were ready and waiting for the ambulance to take us to the depot where we met two Nursing Sisters from No. 3 Canadian General Hospital. They too were volunteers. The four of us crawled into one of the small coaches attached to a troop train. Just as we were about to pull out, two Air Force Officers asked if there might be room for them in our coach. For the most part we were a quiet crowd, although one of the officers chatted most of the while, even when we all wished that he would be quiet so that we might doze, as our train did not reach Amiens until sometime in the morning. The other was a slightly built, fair-haired boy, with a whimsical smile that played around his mouth, almost as if he might be nervous. He seemed depressed and had little to say. His companion kept ragging him, telling him to "Snap out of it".

When we reached Amiens, Lieutenant Knight suggested that we go with him to a Scottish hospital, quite close by the depot, for a cup of tea. He knew that we would be welcome even at 5 a.m. We were truly grateful to these charming Scottish girls for their hospitality. We had to go from Amiens by transport to a small village fifteen miles away, where we would be picked up by the hospital train. Lieutenant Knight

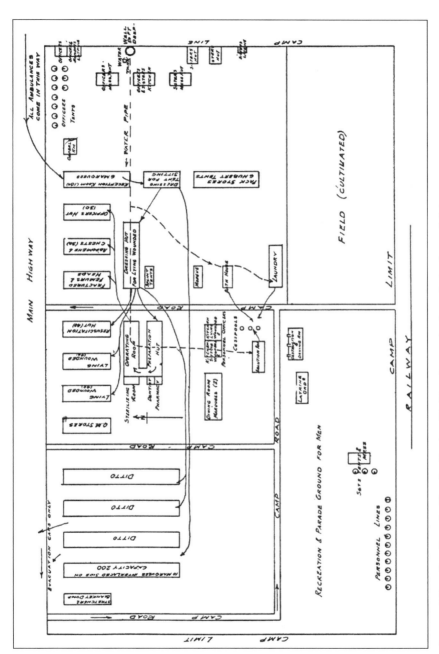

Layout of Canadian Casualty Clearing Station. Working close to the front, during heavy fighting.

came along that far with us, looking after our travelling vouchers and luggage. He seemed to be such a young boy to be wearing his Wings. Thanking him, we said goodbye when the train drew in. He told us that he would dip his wings the following morning when his squadron went over our hospital.

This was our first experience on a hospital train, equipped much the same as the hospital ships. The Sisters in charge were Territorials, who chatted away about our work in general as we traveled along. No. 44 Casualty Clearing Station was almost at the door of the improvised depot. Starting off to find the Matron, we turned a corner and almost ran into a Medical Officer coming on the fly. When we stopped directly in front of him to ask directions, he took one look at our Canadian badges and a broad grin broke out all over his face. In a perfectly normal Canadian accent he exclaimed "Well, Holy smoke", and we knew that we had found a friend in camp. Asking him where we would likely find the Matron, he replied, "Well at the moment, she is on an inspection tour with seventeen generals and a sergeant", and off he flew. As we passed one of the marquee doors a Nursing Sister came out with one of the most weary faces I have ever seen. Telling her that we were "The Relief" she welcomed us with open arms. She said that she had been on duty for thirty hours. Not much wonder that she was glad we had come. Noticing a General, Colonel and Sergeant departing, we knew that now we might go and find the Matron. I must confess my heart was skipping a beat here and there as I remembered the Matron of the British General Hospital at Versailles, the last British Matron we had reported to. We were in for a very pleasant surprise.

The Matron of No. 44 Casualty Clearing Station, was a small, slightly built woman, wearing the scarlet cape of the Q.A.I.M.N.S. Her hair was almost pure white, her checks pink, and she had the softest blue eyes. We felt immediately we would be glad to serve under this frail looking little woman. The only fly in the ointment was the fact that we were to be separated. Sister Willett was to go on duty immediately, I to bed to have a sleep, and be ready for duty at 7 p.m. - Did I say bed? When the Matron was giving us our orders, she said that she would see that an orderly would take some biscuits to our tent, as well as bedding. Biscuits, biscuits? What ever did she mean, at 11 a.m.? If we were to be parted, at least we were to share the same sleeping quarters. When an orderly, laden down with blankets and four small mattresses, came to our door I understood.

"Your biscuits Sister". We both laughed. We had both been wondering why we were being served biscuits at that hour. While Willett made haste to get into her service uniform, I made up the biscuits. They looked very much like single bed mattresses cut in two. We placed and held them together by tucking the sheet firmly around both. There were no cots, so our beds were made up on the ground, on top of a tarpaulin that was used as a flooring.

"Goodbye old dear, sweet dreams", Willet called back as she left for the hospital.

After the previous days' hard work and travelling all night, and regardless of the fact that my biscuit was very thin and the ground very hard, I was soon fast asleep. I was wakened very suddenly by the noise of an explosion that was repeated and again followed by other terrific blasts. I sat up in bed, realizing I was having my first taste of gun fire at close range. I began to wonder if the hospital was being bombed. I even felt a bit resentful that Willett had not come to waken me - Waken me! As if I would need anyone to waken me with that thunderous noise going on. Deciding I would rather take it standing up, I got up and dressed, then took a look outside. No excitement there. One of the sisters who could not sleep, saw me up and dressed and came to reassure me that this was an everyday occurrence since The Push had begun. We had happened to arrive in the lull of the guns. This Sister had been on duty on the ward, a wooden hut, that I was to take over. She was being transferred back to the base, as her nerves were bothering her.

Sister Thomas gave me a vivid picture of the horrors I might expect. The only ward in the camp fitted out with good beds was in a wooden hut. The marquees were equipped with stretchers only, as the Casualty Clearing Station was only a stop gap between the trenches and the ambulance trains. The patients were moved rapidly after their arrival at No. 44. If it was known that a boy had only a few hours to live or his condition was critical, and there was a vacant bed in the hut, it was given to him. It was really a very fine arrangement. Many times in the night to come, I would wish that the parents had known their boy had at least the comfort of a decent bed, and a Padre standing by for his last few hours. My heart ached, for they were so very young, and very brave. Surely they had deserved something better than to be snuffed out at so early an age - "Just fodder for guns". There were only ten sisters allowed at the Casualty Clearing Station, owing to the fact that we were only five miles behind the firing line. There was always the danger that the enemy might make a push forward, in which case the fewer women there were, the better for all concerned. The Matron even suggested that at all times we carry a tube of morphine in our pockets. She felt it would be better for us to take an overdose than to be captured by the Germans, but she left it to us whether to accept her advice or not. As a matter of fact, I never did.

The first night, I received my orders from a Territorial Nursing Sister, one of the finest women I have ever been privileged to work with. I was always glad, in the morning, to leave my boys under her care, as her very manner had a soothing effect. What a ward of horrors! Out of forty-eight beds, possibly ten might live to see the base hospital. As far as possible the ward was classified into sections; amputations, chest, abdominal, and head cases. Perhaps the head cases were the most harrowing. A boy would come in with all his senses, and suddenly I would hear a scream, and would find that he had gone absolutely insane, often with all his bandages torn off, and his wound hemorrhaging, with particles of his brain oozing out of the open wound. Immediately he would be moved to an empty tent. Always I prayed that the end would come soon, and mercifully. If ever a time could come that a merciful shot might be tempted, it was then. Every second we must be ready for an emergency. It was a great responsibility for only one sister and an orderly to accept. The fact that we were so very much needed gave us the strength to carry on and give of our very best.

Sister Bothwell had given me a history of each patient. Private Gordon, an abdominal case, while he suffered no pain, had become paralyzed, and he had not long to live. Often I felt that it was cruel to have him in that ward, with so much agony all around on every side. Yet he did have a decent bed. Beside him lay an amputation case and, as he tossed and moaned, Private Gordon would reach out his hand and take the hand of the suffering boy and I would hear him say "Steady pal, just hold on awhile more". It was always this way. When I became bitter, as I often did, and even doubted that there could be a God, I had only to witness what went on in that ward to come down off my high horse and see Christ by every bedside. They were so unselfish, so patient, so very brave, so very young.

The first night that I was on duty four of my boys had "gone west" as the boys put it. As the end drew near screens were drawn around the beds, and we tried to make the end, the last few hours, as easy as it was possible for us to do. One lad, who looked as if he might be eighteen years of age, asked me to write to his wife and baby. He had been wounded bringing in his friend from "No Man's Land". They occupied beds close to each other and, as they lived and fought together, so they went out together. I closed their eyes and brushed back the hair from their now untroubled brows, and folded their hands. They were wrapped in their gray army blankets, then carried out into the clear night. No more would the guns that thundered disturb their peace. Later the following day, they would be laid to rest with the many others, a kind Padre reading the burial service while all around the sun would shine down on the growing field of wheat and scarlet poppies that swayed in the morning breeze.

As the very gray dawn appeared, I heard overhead the droning of aeroplanes. I remembered what Lieutenant Knight had said. I took time to go to the door. In the east, over the firing line, I could still see star shells flashing like fireworks. I thought of the four boys lying in their last sleep and the fragments of humanity still restlessly tossing on beds of pain; war victims, shell shocked and torn. With a great hate in my heart I silently called to the men guiding their planes, "Good luck, Lieutenant Knight, toss your bomb over swift and straight." The following day on the daily casualty list was the name of Lieutenant Knight, "Killed while on active service".

The days were passing with fierce fighting on the Somme front, one night of horror following another. The mornings found us tired beyond words, ready to lie down on our little mattresses on the ground and sleep the sleep of the utterly weary, regardless of the black beetles that wandered at will over our coverlets and faces. (I always had loathed creeping creatures.) The thunder of the guns had ceased to bother us. However, I did have a grievance with an Officer from the Lord Strathcona's Horse, Winnipeg Regiment who had been sent over to No. 44 Casualty Clearing in charge of a company of ambulance men, to relieve the overworked orderlies. While his men were on duty in the afternoon, he employed his time exercising his horse in a field opposite the Sisters' sleeping quarters. Round and round he galloped. I could not sleep, I made every circuit of the field with him. It seemed so silly to be kept awake by the feet of a galloping horse when the guns never disturbed me.

I soon learned that, with all the work and worry of my ward at No. 44, there were always some bright spots. One was Colonel Shaw, the Surgeon-in-Chief of the operating hut. For the first two days of the big push he had stood operating, scarcely taking time for refreshments, drinking cups of black coffee as a stimulant. At last he dropped and had to be carried out, to rest his mind and body. When he recovered well enough to be back on duty, he came every night to visit his patients. He was a very tall man, with gray hair and stooped shoulders. Once he came with his arms full of flowers, because he said that he felt my ward needed cheer more than any other in the camp. He would go from bed to bed, talking to each man. The soft burr of his Scottish tongue had the soothing effect of a sedative. Always he would say before leaving, "Sister, they have suffered enough, give them rest". So quieting an effect had he on the men that it would not be necessary to administer the prescribed sedative for an hour or more. I felt that he was the most Christ-like man I had ever met.

Early one morning an Officer came to my door.

"Sister, I am bringing in a German prisoner."

In an instant I was up in arms. I looked down the row of wounded men, victims from the fire of German guns. I decided I just could not do it.

"Nurse a Hun? Captain McLean, is it not asking a lot of me?" The Captain just looked at me.

"Sister he is only a boy". He looked so disappointed in me that I consented, but with very poor grace, I fear. They brought him in, a dark-haired boy, who looked more like a frightened schoolboy than a grown man and a soldier. He was suffering from a terrible abdominal wound. One look at his terrified face and he was no longer a hated Hun, just a small wounded boy without a friend on any side. What hurt the most was the fact that he was frightened of me. When I slipped my arm under his head to give him a drink of water, he looked up into my face and smiled, then caught my hand and kissed it. I could not keep the tears from my eyes. Captain McLean, standing at the foot of the cot, turned away and said "Thank you". I felt that he knew he was safe in leaving his wounded with me. We worked hard that night to save the boy's life, although we knew from the beginning that it was a losing game. What good sportsmanship the men in the ward showed. Once, when I asked the orderly to get me an extra pillow, at least four in the surrounding beds offered their one and only pillow. Dawn had still not come when the tired eyes lost their frightened expression and closed. My heart felt sorry for a mother in Germany. I wished that she might have known that a kindly priest had stood by her little boy until the last, and the Nursing Sister had nothing but pity in her heart. His helplessness and youth had wiped away all hate. Possibly in peacetime or ordinary life these men were rather uncouth or illiterate, yet in the days of a bitter war, each one had stood up and they were real men and heroes.

Often in the passing days I had been thankful for a Paddy or Pat in my ward, so here I was once more glad for my Irish boy, and he was only a boy after all. He had come in shell shocked and with a hemorrhaging amputated limb, so weak from loss of blood that he was in a very critical condition. Paddy was young with plenty of reserve strength. Soon we knew that he had a fighting chance. With his returning strength, his spirits rose. From Cork, Ireland, he was typically Irish - his spirits either up in the air or down in the depths. One evening when he had been particularly "down", I rumpled his tousled head, suggesting that he cheer up, because he would soon be leaving the base hospital, and going home to Cork.

"But Sister, without me leg, U'll be no good at all, at all." I went on to assure him that he would be provided with a very fine leg and soon he would be walking the same as ever again. Paddy's black eyes snapped.

"I'm glad o' that, Sister." I was satisfied that I had routed him out of his depression for a spell at least.

"Sure, Sister it will be fine, I'll jist wak into my Mither's house, sit down and screw me leg off, it will be a grand surprise that I will be giving her". He chuckled with the very thought of it. The Commanding Officer appeared just at that moment. The Colonel was a typically

British, Imperial Medical Officer, and often appeared very stern and forbidding. Paddy hailed him with a congenial air. "Even'n Kernel, sure sister tells me I will be git'n meself a new leg to walk on". Even the sickest tried to keep their amusement hidden. As the Colonel stopped at the foot of Paddy's bed, was it only imagination, or did I really see a twinkle in the blue eyes, as he wished Paddy "Goodnight and good luck".

One morning Sister Fitzgerald waited for me at the breakfast table and suggested that I join her on a trip up to Albert. The Paymaster had to go up on business and had offered to take a couple of the sisters for the drive. That is, as far as they would be allowed to go. Of course we knew that what was left of Albert would be out of bounds for women at least. Knowing that it would mean only a little over an hour that we would be away from camp, we accepted his invitation to go as far as we would be allowed, then wait for the return of the transport. We knew that it would be interesting and besides, we would be glad to get away from the hospital for a short breathing spell.

At the breakfast table I had picked up an English paper on the front page of which was printed a short poem entitled "Splashes of Blood", written by a soldier in France. He described the poppies that grew in abundance everywhere, in the valleys, on the hillsides, as symbolizing "splashes of blood" on his fallen comrades. As I read it I thought how horribly gruesome it was, but it seemed to stick in my mind. When the big transport stopped to pick us up we were waiting by the roadside. Soon we were rolling along the country road, leaving a trail of dust in our wake. France is beautiful, and especially in the country. We were headed for Albert, a distance of five miles away. Soon we came to the first evidence of war at close range, the trenches that were already dug and prepared for a push back, with rolls and rolls of barbed wire. What a preparation, trenches and more trenches. At one spot we came close to horses, hundreds of them, patiently standing or cropping the long grass under the trees in a field close to the road. A Cavalry Brigade. The Sergeant did not seem to know why the horses had been brought up so close to the firing line. (The horses never were used in actual battle. The Cavalry volunteered to fight with the infantry, and had done so.) At one point he pointed out the tower that had been the German objective for many hours that same week. It was crumpled and battered, and we marveled that it was still standing after the hours of constant shelling. To us it was all very interesting. For the moment the guns were quiet, so we felt comparatively safe to look around us. Coming down into the valley we saw poppies blooming on every side of us, making great blotches of red in the green grass. "Splashes of blood" drummed through my brain. I looked to one side and there they were - "splashes of blood". I tried to fight off a feeling of nausea, shut my eyes so that I would not see them. Sister Fitzgerald, chatting away, turned to say something to me. "Sister are you ill?" She must have thought that I had gone mad, when I replied, "Yes, I see splashes of blood in the grass." With some water, provided from the Sergeant's water bottle, I soon got hold of myself, and once more we were on our way. But I kept my eyes "front" after that.

It was a busy road, such big business this war had become. Every moment we were passing huge army trucks carrying loads of material and rations for the men. Several times we passed ammunition dumps, and the ever familiar gray ambulances, coming along in a steady stream. Nearer to Albert we met a battalion of men coming back out of the trenches to rest billets. On so many faces was that tense expression, telling the tale of what they had been through. Along the roadside exhausted men lay sleeping. We were very much surprised that we had not been stopped. Possibly we were overlooked by the sentry, thinking that no woman would be fool enough to go so close to the firing line, and we sat well back in our sheltered truck cab. Even before we came to the village we decided to go as far as they would allow us, and did get directly into the little war-torn town, a shattered place. We passed the Cathedral or what was left of it, with the marble statue of the Virgin still hanging aslant from the steeple top. The French people always believed that when the statue actually fell the war would end.

We were possibly the only women to come so dangerously close to the front line trenches. What puzzled us most was to see so many observation balloons (sausages) left hanging in the air after the shelling of the past three weeks. I think perhaps the Sergeant was the most relieved man in the British army when he had us on the road headed for camp. It was possibly a case of "Fools walking where Angels feared to tread". It had never occurred to us that at any moment a stray shell might come sailing in our direction. That very night a shell did come, passing directly over the hospital, and tearing a great crater in the wheat field just beyond us. At the time I was carrying a wide tray piled high with dressings and equipment. For the first time I lost my nerve. The tray, solutions, instruments and dressings went crashing to the floor, while I stood in a daze. It was the one and only shell we ever had any experience with during our stay at No. 44 Casualty Clearing Station. The Germans must have heard of our visit to Albert, and sent along their shell as a warning.

Sister Willett's and my return call came during the night. We were both worn out. However, it was with regret that we said farewell to the nursing staff of No. 44 British Casualty Clearing Station. We realized the English Nursing Sisters were not so reserved and cold as we had felt in the beginning. We were driven the seventeen miles to Amiens where we got the train for the Boulogne train and came home to No. 3 Canadian Stationary Hospital at the base.

The great Somme push commenced July 1st, 1916. That day 60,000 casualties were listed dead and wounded. It was never a complete success, dragging on for weeks without reaching its objective, Bapaume. Here too, for the first time, the new Tank Corps went into action, one of the war's first surprises. No one could imagine such an invention, weighing thirty tons, a steel monster enclosing the guns and with a long, swaying tail. On September 15th, 1916, on a misty morning, they made their first charge, astonishing and scaring the very daylights out of their own troops, as well as those of the foe. The tanks had been hidden so well, even our own men did not know that they existed.

On our arrival at our own hospital everything seemed to be so peaceful. We were looking forward to a good night's sleep, free from the roar of the guns. But luck was against us. Between midnight and 2 a.m. we were wakened with what sounded exactly like a bombardment, only later learning that an ammunition dump had been bombed at Calais. Possibly the reaction of weeks of service up at the front, my nerves were giving me trouble. Our Matron, quick to notice anything amiss with her Nursing staff, shipped Willett and me off for two weeks leave, and a change as well as a rest. Our first official leave since departing Canada.

Willett and I felt like two school girls let out to play, as we started off, deciding to forget hospitals and army duty for a whole fourteen days. We spent the first night at the Wampach Hotel in Folkestone, revelling in the luxury of real beds and lavender scented bed linen. The sweet tones of a church bell wakened us in the morning. It was the Sabbath day. We would have an early breakfast, and a walk around the small town, maybe even down on the Leas, then attend a church service. We were off to a good start. The sun was shining after the habitual rain we had been having in France. Stepping out into the warm sunshine, we were off to explore places. Almost the first thing that we saw was a Canadian battalion out on route march. Swinging along with full equipment, they sang as they marched "It's a Long Way to Tipperary." So many Canadian boys had never come back. As we watched them pass by we wondered if this was the regiment the English woman had warned her neighbor to run from. Sister Walker, on returning from leave, in the Sisters' mess had told the following yarn as a good joke on the Canadian boys. "A regiment of Canadians camped in the vicinity of Folkestone, out on route march were surprised when, turning into a narrow street on the outskirts of the town, they saw a woman who had been standing gossiping with her neighbors throw up her arms and take to her heels, shouting as she ran, "Take to your 'omes, here come the Canadians on the rampage!'"

We heard the church bell calling all good people to come and worship. The church where we decided to attend divine worship was a small Anglican one. The architecture told the story of how old it must be, a hundred years or more. Very dignified and peaceful it looked, with the sunshine streaming in through the lead pane, amber glass windows. The mellow rays fell across the rich dark wood of the interior furnishings. The sweet tones of the pipe organ welcomed the people as they took their places in the quaint, high-back pews. We found that we were the only occupants of the seat we were shown to. It was interesting to watch the people, away from the hurrying throngs of the mixed military in France. Here were mostly women or older men. What young men there were, were mostly in khaki. Many of the women were in deep mourning. I could not help hoping that the women of Canada would be wise enough to dispense with the customary deep mourning. Never did our countries need cheer as they did then, if only in the colour of their wearing apparel, in these dark days of war. My wandering thoughts lead to the example Harry Lauder had set. He was about

Scenes from France. Top: Capt. Scott, Sisters Johnston, Neelands, Prichard, Carr, and Capt. Hillier, CAMC. Lower Left: Sisters Kidd and Deason. Lower Right: Kate Wilson gathering flowers for her Ward.

to make his first appearance on the stage, when he was handed a telegram informing him of the death of his only son, "Killed while on active service". When a friend suggested that he postpone his engagement he straightened up. "No," he said, "My son would never have wished me to fail the boys". With his heart torn by the tragic news, he went on with the performance and never faltered once.

The entry of the choir, singing its way up the aisle roused me from my reveries. We did not know, both being Presbyterians, that this was a special service, beseeching special blessing and prayers for the safety of the whole Royal family, starting with our Gracious King George V, repeating in order his Christened names, and on down to the youngest member of the family. As the names were repeated in a chanting tone of voice, I thought, what a lot of nonsense. Surely the good Lord would have been satisfied equally as well to have been asked to keep and guard the Royal family - or, for that matter, the whole Empire, that was suffering and dying for us. Anyway, it would have saved a lot of valuable time, and we might have listened to something more interesting.

Monday morning we left for London, where we intended to visit before going on to Lydd to visit Sister Willett's brother, in training at a Canadian camp there. It had been a year since we had visited London. So much had happened in the intervening time. I had almost forgotten its crowded streets and ancient buildings. Comparing it with Paris and Cairo, we decided from an historical point of view that we found it much more interesting. We also knew that we could never cover it in the time we had at our disposal. There were three or four places that might be of special interest. We would visit these and leave the rest for a future date. Madame Tussaud's we made our starting point, and we were not disappointed in our choice. From the stooped old lady dressed in black and sitting at the entrance, to the gruesome dens in the basement, it was thrilling. Nothing of importance in the world's notables or up-to-date events had been missed, from the large sand map of the Panama Canal to the Western front trenches. It was all there, the development of each from the beginning. This must have necessitated the continual changing of the map of the "front" trenches almost every day. It was all very amazing. Famous people in life-sized statues, so real one could almost see them breathing. Queen Victoria, Florence

Nightingale, Victor Hugo, Bismarck, Marie Antoinette, Madame Pompadour and many, many more. So lifelike were these statues that at one point I got a shock, standing looking at a Canadian soldier dressed in khaki, who stood facing the front door. I was on the verge of going over to see what he was labeled with, when a broad smile broke out all over his face as two of his friends entered the door to join him. He turned and gave me a wicked wink.

There was such a fund of information to be gathered, if only we had time to study the history of everything; the ancient carriages, suits of armour, models of ships, such as the Mayflower, groups of interesting events that were familiar to all of us. There were the signing of the Magna Carta, the execution of Mary Queen of Scots (so real it made one weep); the capture of Quebec, the death of Wolfe. As well as these there were the many gruesome objects of the dark ages, that made one glad to be living in the year 1916. We saw horrible forms of ancient punishments for criminals, even the "stocks". One might go on for hours, viewing these clever works of the wax moulders. The work was so fine in colour and detail that even the lace trimming on some of the garments had a fluffy, sheer appearance. Particularly did we notice that in the high ruffle of the gown of Queen Elizabeth I. By the time we finished we were surprised to note that the day was almost gone. Later these wax works were burned to the ground. They were rebuilt and new figures replaced those destroyed. I wonder if it was exactly the same. At least we are still glad that we saw the original.

The Tower of London held a store of information, right from the ancient arch entry, through which so many broken hearts have passed, still guarded by the Beefeaters in their colourful costumes of red and black. They wore the emblem of the thistle, rose and shamrock embroidered on the front of their bloused tunics, high ruffled lace collars, and wide brimmed hats. They looked as if they might have stepped out of the fourteenth century. From Wakefield Tower, where the crown jewels are stored, our interest never lagged. The Crown jewels, closely guarded by the King's soldiers, held our rapt attention. It was almost unbelievable, the wealth that had been collected behind those heavy glass walls, from the Royal Crown to the most insignificant bracelet. The beauty and design were perfect. Most of the adornments looked very cumbersome. I felt sorry for the person who might be obliged to wear them.

Many years before, while studying English history, I had wept for the two fair-haired English boys, who had been unfortunate enough to be born Princes, and were brutally murdered in the upper room of the Tower of London. I never dreamed that I would climb the narrow stone stairway and stand in the small room, with its small barred windows, where they met their doom, nor that I would visit the place where the beautiful Mary Queen of Scots thanked her devoted Lady in Waiting before she knelt to be beheaded. It was almost too terrible to think about. We were glad to leave those rooms, with their tragic stories of so many years ago. Yet even in those days, we remembered that the Tower of London continued its brutal repetition of history. For it was there that many spies met their deaths before a firing squad, instead of the beheading block. Perhaps it may have all been a part of discipline, but it was still brutal.

On our third day we started out to visit Hyde Park and Kensington Gardens. Taking an omnibus, we climbed to the very top, so that we might not miss anything in the passing. We got off at the place that we had been directed to, or at least we thought we did. Being in a strange land we were very much confused when we found we had made a mistake. Not seeing a policeman in sight we started to walk and, coming to a small bookstore we decided to go in and ask just where we were. We were waited on by a small man with smooth fair hair, slicked down and very shiny, who looked over the top of his glasses at us when we made our enquiry.

"Ah yes miss, you have made a mistake. Just a five minutes' walk to the bottom of the street, will get you to your omnibus." Thanking him, we started off to walk, very vague as to how far we might be able to walk in five minutes, or if we would know the bottom of the street when we came to it. After we had gone what we felt was at least a mile, we decided that we had missed our directions again. Once more we appealed for assistance, and we could hardly keep from laughing when we were once more directed, "Just a five minute walk to the bottom of the street." We found out that we were hopelessly ignorant of what the bottom of the street was, or how far an Englishman can walk in five minutes. This time we made sure that we would be able to recognize the omnibus stop when we came to it.

Approaching Victoria Gateway, forming the entrance between Hyde Park and Kensington Gardens, we were delighted with the beauty of our surroundings. Dignified, picturesque, low stone walls, hedges and shrubbery, told of the wealth of the people who dwelt there. Hyde Park is perhaps one of the world's oldest pleasure grounds, covering an area of three hundred and seventy-five acres. Every inch of the ground is a treasure store of English history. From the time it had been the property of the ancient Westminster Abbey, down through the ages, it had undergone many changes, until, in 1916, we were permitted to view it in its maximum state of beauty, with its hills and valleys, historical statuary, and ancient trees, profuse flowers and velvety grass. Standing on one of the small bridges spanning the Serpentine river, to watch the people and admire the scene, and looking down into the clear, flowing water, it was hard to believe that at one time it had been a germ-infested puddle of water. Caroline, Queen of George II had undertaken to have it dredged and converted into a clean healthy stream. We wondered why it had been called Serpentine, with its straight banks built up with stone walls. Despite its beauty I could not help comparing it with the wide, swift running, deep winding and twisting rivers of Canada, with their rocky, wooded banks. In a sense I felt sorry for the artificial grandeur of the English stream.

We found a seat on one of the grassy hillsides, glad to sit and rest awhile. Scarcely were we seated when a park attendant approached us, demanding a "thruppence". Handing him the three pennies, we thought we would get our money's worth of information regarding the park, and he was very obliging. The huge ten story red brick building, visible through the tops of the green trees was the Hyde Park Hotel. The main entrance was in Knightsbridge. This was one of the most fashionable and popular resorts in London. He also told us that a part of the park had been taken over for a playground for both young and old. He told us where to find the most interesting promenades. We got our "thruppence" worth.

As I sat surveying it all I could not help thinking what a vast change it had undergone. We viewed the quiet grounds of the Monastery, which King Henry VIII, in his bombastic manner, abolished and turned into a hunting ground to satisfy his personal pleasure, stocking it with deer, stag and fox. With the amount of hunting that must have been carried on, it is remarkable that these survived so long, for even during the reign of Queen Elizabeth I, they were still to be found in the park. Judging from the history we read, each royal house must have taken an interest in the park, to its advantage or disadvantage. Under King William III and Queen Anne some thirty acres were taken over for Kensington Garden Place. Later Caroline, Queen of George II, who seemed to have been a lady with an eye for beauty, added more to the gardens. Early in the time of Charles I, a part of it was converted into a race track for horses. Imagine the enormous sums of money that had been won and lost in that famous old place. Duellists also found Hyde Park a favorite "Naming place" to settle their grievances. In Cromwell's time it was famous for coach races. Not until the time of Charles II had it developed into a favorite spot for Kings and Queens to ride or drive, or for the fashionable set of London to frequent the promenades. Now in 1916, there was another change.

As we were about to leave the grounds, over the hill came a motley squad of new recruits, returning from practice. More men to meet the enemy in Belgium and France to kill and be killed. It was impossible not to wonder just how far civilization had advanced in the matter of settling differences since the ancient days of the Westminster Monastery. Would there ever come a time when a more sane method of conflict would be adopted by the whole world?

From the admiration my Grandfather Lytle had always held for the hero Nelson, I had a fascination for Trafalgar Square. The enormous Memorial erected to Nelson's memory expressed the love and high esteem his country had for this great sailor. The imposing column rose one hundred and sixty feet high, and contained records of Nelson's four great battles. On the very top stood the statue of Lord Nelson. At the base four lions stood on guard. It was also interesting to remember that this was the spot where famous political gatherings had taken place, as well as riots to gain entrance to irregular meetings. Apart from the Nelson feature, on the north side were the National Galleries and on the north east corner, the church of Martin-In-The-Field. We arrived just in time to see a wedding party coming out of the church, the winsome bride on the arm of her soldier husband. His fellow officers formed an archway with their guns, under which the happy couple passed, while doves fluttered and cooed in admiration.

Our holiday was slipping away. Realizing that London could not be seen in a week or even a month, we were thankful for having been able to visit one or two spots of interest; The Strand, Fleet Street, Drury Lane, and Chancery Lane. All of these we had travelled in our sightseeing; places that echoed the atmosphere of Charles Dickens' books. In fact, there were times when I would not have been surprised to have actually met Oliver Twist, or even Snodgrass himself in one of these haunts. This was especially so in the Cheshire Cheese Inn, with its sawdust covered floors and unattractive solid, ancient furniture. Here we refused the beer, and tried to convince ourselves that we enjoyed the other bill of fare. Walking along the embankment, we passed the Cleopatra's Needle, reminding us of the Obelisks we had seen in Paris and Egypt. It looked very much out of place in the English surroundings with its two Sphinxes standing guard at the foot. It was hard to understand how these huge pillars of stone had been transferred from their native Egyptian land.

Before leaving England we spent several days in the tiny village of Lydd, in Hampshire. It was a quiet, peaceful, typically English village, with many green hedges of pivot, thatched roof houses, and a very old and quaint Anglican church, with a well kept cemetery alongside. While Sister Willett had a visit with her brother I explored the lovely little church, and talked with the friendly people. I was grateful to have found a quiet spot to catch my breath and rest, before we had to say goodbye to England, and once more set sail for France.

Chapter Nine; Editor's Notes

1) The only evidence that remains of the Casualty Clearing Station is the cemetery they used. Puchevillers British Cemetery contains 1,763 Commonwealth and 74 German burials. The German who died on Sister Wilson's watch would certainly be buried there. Her Private Gordon is most probably Rifleman S.M. Gordon, Royal Irish Rifles died of wounds July 3rd, 1916. Sister Wilson served at the 44th CCS from July 3rd to July 20th, 1916.

2) Sister Fitzgerald (Lillian Mary Fitzgerald) was born in Halifax on October 19th, 1889.

3) The leaning Golden Virgin of Albert was one of the most enduring legends of the Great War. It was assumed that when the Virgin fell the war would end (and be lost). Consequently French Engineers secured the statue with cables and it remained in position through 1916-1917. British artillery toppled the Golden Virgin when Albert was lost to the Germans in the Spring of 1918.

4) Harry Lauder was a famous British stage performer. He often entertained the troops and was immensely popular. Lauder's only son was killed on the Somme in December 1916.

Chapter Ten

An American Unit

While waiting to go on board the *Victoria* at Folkestone wharf, we were conscious of an unusual stir. Usually the ship was crowded with Nursing Sisters and Officers returning from leave, priests in their long black clerical gowns and, frequently, a number of military officials. Generally the air was a subdued one. As we walked up the gangway a merry peal of laughter came from the upper deck, making us both smile, especially as we noticed a stern Colonel wearing the red band of Headquarters Staff, turn slowly with a frown on his face to see where all the merriment was coming from. No doubt he thought it was some noisy colonial, and was looking to see whether the disturber of the peace was from Australia or Canada. For once the Colonel was fooled, for it came from neither Imperial nor Colonial, but from a trim looking unit of Red Cross Nursing Sisters from the United States... there was not a thing that he could do about it in the way of discipline.

These Americans were the first that we had come in contact with. To us they were like a breath of fresh air. They looked so smart in their white uniforms and navy capes, the officers in uniforms of khaki. Noticing our Canadian badges, they came over and introduced themselves in their characteristic warm manner. They were a unit from Detroit, Michigan. Soon we were chatting as if we had known them for ages. It was indeed a pleasure to meet these intelligent women, who had volunteered to come over and help us. We were sorry that they were to be stationed near Etaples, and some distance from Boulogne. I knew that to many of these girls it was the greatest thrill of their lives. We wondered how soon the United States would come to help our men, who were holding the lines for all of us. We felt sure that eventually they would join forces with us as Allies.

Half an hour before we landed at Boulogne the skies darkened and the rain came down in torrents. What a weepy country France appeared to be in 1916, rain and still more rain. Slipping on our raincoats we followed the Americans down the gangway, hoping that it was only "au revoir" that they waved as they gathered up their skirts and ran for shelter. Being prepared for the downpour, Sister Willett and I took our way leisurely up the long hill, preferring to walk in the clean rain, rather than take a trolley at a time of day when it would be crowded with French labourers, the majority of them fishermen. We had not forgotten an instance, some short time ago when we had taken a trolley. When we climbed on board it was full to overflowing, so we were forced to stand on the outer platform. Rather than have to wait another half hour, we wedged our way in. There were two stalwart Australians sitting on the outer railing of the tram. Between where we stood and where they were sitting a half dozen French fishermen kept up a baffling chatter, interlaced with boisterous laughter. As the tram slowed down at a curve, one of the men, more rude than the others, gave his companion a shove in our direction, almost knocking us off balance. Quicker than the deed was done, one of the Australians reached over and caught the offender by the back of his collar. Quickly and easily he lifted him off his feet and over the railing and sat him down, both surprised and swearing with rage, on the cobblestone road. He then continued his conversation with his companion, never once looking in our direction. It was when we came in contact with this type of gentleman, that it jarred us to hear someone from the Imperial forces speak in terms of contempt of the undisciplined Australians.

When we reached camp around 7 p.m. we found that several changes had taken place during our absence. Several of the orderlies had transferred to the Infantry or Air Force. A number of fifth year medical students had returned to Canada for their last year of University work. After graduating they would return with their Commissions, and join some hospital or regiment. We learned with real regret of the transfer of our own Padre Frost from France to England. He had always been a vital part of the unit. His going was accompanied with the well wishes of each staff member, as well as congratulations for his approaching marriage to Janet Wilson, from Peterborough, Ontario. Also, his promotion to Major had been granted. This made a complete change in the Chaplain section of our staff, with the exception of Captain Khuring.

It seemed singular we never did call this dignified officer, Padre. Maybe it was this dignity that forbade any term of familiarity. It was always a pleasure to have him visit our wards, this big man with the shock of curly white hair, and a most benevolent face. Rarely did he ever come without gifts for the boys: Home magazines and papers for the colonials, books for the old country boys, and flowers for the sister. One day he came in with a large bowl of black bramble berries he had gathered along the fence at the back of the camp. The scratches on his arms and hands were evidence of his labours. It was Captain Khuring we had to thank for the musical element and effort in camp. Always, he was responsible for an impromptu concert or choir for the Sabbath service. He seemed always able to find someone capable of bringing real music out of our tiny hand organ, while he conducted the singing himself. Possibly our hospital was unique in being the only hospital or camp to have a set of chimes to call us to worship. From four or five pieces of steel cut to various lengths, he had contrived to produce different notes. These lengths were fastened to a wooden bar in such a manner that by striking them with a tiny mallet, they sent forth musical tones. It was a good imitation of a small carillon, and could be heard from every part of the camp ground. No. 3 Canadian Stationary Hospital will always have many pleasant memories of our Anglican Padre, Captain Khuring.

We returned to the unit refreshed and glad to be back to work. But it was uphill work for me. The Casualty Clearing Station had left its mark. Many hours I would lie awake thinking about my ward there. I could not seem to make it a closed book. We were posted to day duty, and soon things were running along in routine order with little excitement, with the exception of an occasional German air raid scare. Usually we were warned by three flickers of the electric lights, and the order, "All lights out immediately". Once more the candles were brought into use for an emergency dressing. There was little to do but sit around and wait for developments. At times we could hear the planes flying high up, on their way to England.

One morning very early, just as daylight was breaking, a solitary German plane passed directly overhead, flying rather low. Being a very curious lot of individuals, we ran outside to see what was going to happen. Shells from the aircraft guns directly behind the hospital were exploding in puffs of white smoke around the departing plane, as he hummed his way through the white clouds, while we stood and watched the performance. I was getting more excited every minute, first for fear that we might hit him, and tumble him down in our midst, then for fear that we might not hit him. Suddenly we were dispersed and ordered inside by an irate officer, who inquired of us if we had any sense at all, or if we were trying to get our blooming blocks knocked off by a piece of flying shrapnel. It had never occurred to us that there would be pieces of metal from the exploding shells in the air. As for the German, he was in much too great a hurry to get back to Germany to bother tossing any retaliatory bombs in his wake. Later we learned that one of the staff of No. 3 Canadian General Hospital had been hit on the shoulder by a piece of shrapnel. Just another curious Canadian.

As the days passed by, reports from the front line trenches were coloured with rumours. Occasionally there would be the hint of an armistice in the near future. Then another lot of boys would bring with them pessimistic reports. Our hopes were blown one way and then another. Frequently, patients were admitted who had been to the base hospitals once or twice, patched up and sent back to the trenches. These were the men that my heart went out to. Sometimes I almost dreaded seeing them recover so rapidly, as it only meant that they had to return to the horror of it all again.

While doing a dressing one night I overheard a conversation between two Scottish Border regiment men. The new patient had just been admitted and was assigned to the bed beside Corporal McDonald of his own company, who had been admitted only a few days previously. Corporal Carr related all that had taken place between the time when Corporal McDonald had been wounded and the time he himself had fallen victim. A silence fell between them and finally Corporal McDonald asked, "What about Mac?".

For two or three moments Corporal Carr hesitated, as if weighing his words, then in the kindest of tones, he turned and said "I am sorry old chap, he has gone west." For some time the Corporal lay perfectly still. Then, looking at the bandages that covered the place where his arm had been amputated at the shoulder, and the cradle at the foot of the bed that protected the amputated limb from the bed clothing, he said in a bitter tone of voice, "What a lucky devil he is." Mac was the Corporal's younger brother.

Tragedies like this one were occurring every day. It all seemed so beastly unnecessary. Many times I had talked to boys who did not have the foggiest idea of what it was all about. They seemed to rest on the fact that the Germans were our enemies, and we hated them and were supposed to kill as many of them as possible.

Before I had been at the Casualty Clearing Station I had often listened to the conversations among the men, and the stories that they brought back with them. Now when they rehearsed their tales, I got as far away as possible, and fought off a fit of nerves, and tried to keep from crying, with all the power that I could muster.

One night I discovered that I had a new problem on my hands. Having made the rounds of the three wards in my charge, taking temperatures and looking the night orders over, I noted that a new patient had been admitted for observation. Canadian mail had come in that day and, with a feeling of satisfaction I had patted the bundle of letters in my pocket, making a mental note that I would devour them if I had a lull in the night. Passing through the marquees where there were several Canadian boys, I noticed on their lockers newspapers from home. One boy laughingly remarked that now the papers had arrived from home, they would have some idea of what was happening in the front line trenches. I just laughed, my mind on the observation case. I returned to my order book, to make sure I had not overlooked some order for this particular patient, as he struck me as being a very healthy specimen. When I went to his cot it was empty. None of the men around seemed to be able to give me any information about him, other than that he had pulled on an army blue robe and walked out. One wag suggested that he might have gone to the "Pest" ward to be "Smit". It had been a standing joke about the number of men ready to be dismissed, who had been found in the infectious ward. I was at a loss to know what to do. I made enquiries at the Measles ward but he had not been there, according to the burly armed private at the door. My ward orderlies made a tour of the grounds without finding a trace of the man. Knowing that I was responsible for my wards, I reported to the Night Orderly Officer, a newcomer to the unit staff. He did not help my feelings any by taking a grave look at the whole affair. Hour after hour passed and still the cot remained empty.

The following morning Sister Willett and I, returning from our daily walk, found Charlie, my orderly, waiting for me, to inform me that the lost had been found and to put my mind at rest. In his own peculiar manner of speech he related the discovery.

"Sister, I thought that there was something goofy about that boy, so Herbie and I decided that we would do a bit of detective work on our own. We took a stroll down to the pub in the valley, and there he was, drunk as a lord, so we brought him back to camp." For once I was not worried whether the fellow would get first field punishment or not at the detention camp. That day my sleep was not very peaceful. I would doze off to discover half a dozen of my patients had gone off and were tearing through the trees of happy valley, while I became weary trying to catch up with them. I would waken with a start, take a look at my watch, discover that it was only 11 a.m., turn over and proceed to chase more phantoms.

At the end of our night duty term, we were given a day off duty. This we spent by taking a trolley a couple of miles south of Boulogne, out into a country lovely with the first autumn tints. Here, not far from where Charles Dickens wrote "The Tales of Two Cities", we found a delightful rambling old house where they served *a la carte* dinners. We were away from the hospital, and we could fill our lungs with fresh air, and forget about fleeing patients. The day was warm enough to have afternoon tea in the "rose garden", although there was not a single rose left blooming at that time of year. A long tramp through a lovely woods gave us a hearty appetite for dinner, before we caught the trolley back to camp, arriving just as the bugler announced, "Lights out".

The Day I Met my Future Husband

It had been just one of those days, from Reveille to Taps. At 6 a.m. the bugler's blast, from just outside our tent door, started the day off wrong for me. It had rained all night. By the time I reached the Sisters' mess hut, my white apron and clean fresh uniform were soaked almost to my knees from the long grass that grew on either side of the pathway, and it was too late to go back and change. In the post operative ward where I was in charge, the night orderly had forgotten to empty ash trays or do any other cleaning, so the place looked a fright. There were forty-eight dressings to be done, supplies to be looked after, and continuous drip bath containers to be refilled with heated saline, all before the Orderly Officer for the day made his rounds. In the connecting operating room an emergency case had come in and a dose of cocaine had been administered but the patient proved allergic to the drug, and had gone completely berserk. With one unholy scream he sent basins containing solutions, sterile instruments and mops in all directions. Bandages, scalpels and other equipment covered the floor. The scrubbed surgeon, his assistant, Nursing Sister and orderly tried to hold the casualty on the table. With a limited supply of sterile instruments and other supplies, it meant one grand scramble for the post operative sister to come to the rescue, to resterilize, and replenish the supply of dressings, mops, and bandages. This was one time I realized my operating room technique was far from perfect. I did my best, and trusted in the Grace of God, plus a generous application of iodine, that the patient might survive... he did.

A Sergeant came through calling, "All patients must be ready by 5 p.m. instead of 7 p.m..." another rush. By 4 p.m. the ambulances had arrived, and were waiting with the stretchers for our evacuees. I had the thankful feeling that the day, with all its frustrations, would soon be over. Then Charlie, the orderly, came on the run from the equipment room.

"Sister, those four pairs of partial denture plates, I have got them all mixed up, and can't find the tags, what will I do?" At that time of day, with most of the jaw cases bandaged beyond articulation, I had to think quickly.

"Charlie, walk down the ward, take a good look at each jaw case, and make a good guess." Charlie was off on a trot, his crossed fingers held high over his head. Finally the waiting ambulances were loaded with our stretcher cases, each wearing an improvised toque of yellow, pink or green, made from our supply of Australian bed socks. Thanks and goodbyes were called back as they started on their way to the boats and England, all happy to be going. The dentures? We never knew the finish of that story.

At last I breathed a sigh of relief, as I sat down to fill out my history sheets and the report for the day. Glancing out the window I saw the Colonel pass by, accompanied by a very handsome Canadian Army officer. I was surprised when they turned in at my door.

"Sister Wilson, a friend to see you". I was sure that there must be some mistake, I had never seen this particular officer before. But no, the Lieutenant came walking in, his hand outstretched.

"I believe that you knew my sister, Jean Simmie, in Owen Sound."
Like a flash I remembered the broad shouldered defenseman of the
Wiarton Redmen Hockey team.

"Then you are Rob Simmie, the hockey player?"

Colonel Davis wore a broad grin as he turned to leave. I had just met
my future husband, it had truly been just one of those days.

October had been a month of dreary days and black nights. We put
on our greatcoats and sat huddled around a small round "Perfection"
coal oil stove in our tents, and tried to keep warm. We pitied the boys
in the trenches, failing to see how they ever lived through the cold rain
and filth... and the end of the war seemed as far away as it had months
ago.

The winged songsters of northern France had all vanished, and the
trees had lost their colourful autumn foliage. The camp ground was a
mess of wet mud. I was back on the post-operative ward, more fortunate than most of the Sisters, who had to wear their long rubber boots
and raincoats, plus Souwesters that resembled the caps the fishermen
wore. These they wore from 7 a.m. until 7 p.m. I had a wooden floor
under my feet, and a wooden roof over my head. I could shed my outdoor garments in comfort. In fact, my ward looked very festive. The
Matron had sent over an issue of bright, scarlet woollen blankets, as
well as soft, scarlet flannel nightingale jackets for each one of the
patients. These were most gratefully received as was the comfort that
they brought. The colour added a note of cheer to the dull walls of the
ward. Winter seemed to be just around the corner. The dispatch riders
of the Motorcycle Corps travelling the Calais road past the hospital at
all hours of the day or night bowed their heads in the face of the western wind.

One night early in November, 1916, Willett and I came off our
wards into the black night. The rain was pouring down and we splashed
through puddles of water on our way to the Mess hut, and were glad of
the hot dinner that was served. In our sleeping tent we found that the
sides of our tent bulged with every blast of wind that came tearing
down the hillside, while the guy ropes creaked and groaned, straining
to hold the tent in place. Long before the bugler had sounded "Last
Post", we were wrapped in our heavy woollen dressing robes, with a
steaming hot water bottle for a bed fellow, and tucked into our army

cots. While the rain beat a tattoo on the outer walls of the canvas tent, I lay listening to the howling wind until it lulled me to sleep. Sometime between midnight and 4 a.m. I was wakened by the creaking noise of the centre pole of the tent. A cold wind was swirling around my head. As I reached for my flash-light, I discovered that the guy ropes had given way on one side of the tent. In the watery ray of light, I could see the centre pole standing at a dizzy angle.

"What will we do?" wailed Willett from somewhere under her blankets.

"What can we do?" I asked through the noise of the terrific wind outside. We could hear our next door neighbours laughing. From somewhere we heard a scream: "Heavens our tent's gone". Just then the side of our own tent went down like a puff ball. Away went the tent pole, and we were buried under a sheet of clammy wet canvas.

"Billy, where are you?" called my roommate.

I answered with a muffled, "Here".

We could hear several of the sisters picking their way over fallen tents and guy ropes en route to the mess hut. We decided to stay just where we were until daylight.

"Who ever started this fool war? Sure we will all be drowned!" called out a voice with an Irish accent, as Pat scrambled around outside in the dark and wet.

As soon as it was light enough, we untangled ourselves from the wet folds of canvas and joined the party in the mess hut. Several of the tents had been completely flattened while the others looked as if they had certainly had "a blighty". However the wind had gone down, and streaks of pink in the eastern sky promised a fine day.

In the mess hut we found the sisters in all stages of repair and disrepair. Sister Gee sat with her head covered with a crown of curl papers. We never would have believed we could catch her in that undignified state of body or mind. When Reveille rang out shrill and clear in the cold morning air, Sister Pat, wrapped in a gray flannel blanket up to her chin, sat huddled in a heap, as close to the small stove as she could get, no doubt feeling, as well as looking, half dead. She remarked in her dry tone of voice, "It is Last Post that he should be playing for all of us."

I found that I had lost my voice, I was in the grip of an acute attack of laryngitis. Sister Willett too had developed a cold. The fact that the mess hut was leaking and cold did not help matters. We had dug out enough clothing from the wreck of our tent, and went on duty. We were both called to the Matron's office and told that, owing to our severe colds, we were being sent over to the Princess Louise Convalescent Hospital for Nursing Sisters. This was several miles out in the country west of Boulogne, and we were to remain there until we were fully recovered. We were annoyed as well as amused, as we did not really feel ill enough to be sent off duty. However, orders are orders in the army, so off we went.

The Princess Louise Hospital turned out to be the hunting-box of the Duke of Argyle, taken over by the British War Office for the duration, for sick nursing sisters. It was a picturesque, long low building, with several wide verandahs, and many lead paned swinging windows. It was situated at the foot of an incline and was reached by entering between two very lovely stone pillars and wide wrought iron gates. The whole place seemed to be completely surrounded with huge pine trees. A rosy-cheeked boy scout opened the door in answer to our knocking, and invited us to come in. The entrance hall was almost square. An open stairway led off to the left, and directly facing the entrance, a bright fire burned in an open fireplace, over which hung a large oil painting, a hunting scene. A large brown dog was lying in front of the fire, on a large leopard skin rug. As we stood waiting he slowly rose, stretched himself indifferently and walked toward us. He resembled a dane although his coat was much lighter in colour. He had the air of an aristocrat. Always having loved dogs, I held out my hand and went to pat him. He stood looking at me for a moment with intelligent eyes, then, as if he approved, he came and leaned his head against my knee. We learned to love this Russian dog, Mouski.

It was rather late by the time we arrived and we were shown immediately to our room by a white-capped maid, who later brought us our supper on a tray. Although not very large, our room was very comfortable, bright with gay coloured chintz on the bed and chairs. Quite early the following morning we were wakened by a gentle tap on the door. We were surprised to see quite an elderly lady dressed in a white uniform enter, followed by a Boy Scout, with our breakfast. She sat down and talked with us, and had such a winning smile that we fell in love with her. Later in the day we were formally introduced to her, she was

Scenes from France, 1916. Top: Sisters Kidd and Deason near Boulogne. Middle Left: Sisters Willet and Deason. Middle Right: Sister Potter. Bottom: Sisters Kidd and Willett.

Lady Gifford. We were all under her charge with Lady Seymour as her assistant. Before leaving she told us that lunch would be served in the main dining room. In the meantime there was nothing for us to to but enjoy ourselves. One good thing about this compulsory trip, at least we were not to be confined to our beds.

In the living room downstairs there were fifteen or twenty girls sitting around the fireplace. It was a most attractive room, with polished hardwood floors covered with bright scatter rugs. There were deep, comfortable chairs and, at one end of the large room, a beautiful grand piano. On this stood a bowl of bronze mums. On the creamy coloured walls there were several sepia coloured etchings. The whole room was interesting and inviting. There were girls from South Africa, Australia, New Zealand, England and, of course, the Canadians.

There were very few rules to abide by, the strictest being that we have our breakfast in bed. Also, we must have a medical once a week. Each day lunch was served in the dining room, where two long tables were laid. At one were seated all the girls from the colonies, and Lady Gifford graced the head of the table. At the other table sat the girls from England and Lady Seymour presided. Afternoon tea was served in the living room. We found the nurses of the colonies so easy to become acquainted with, the Australians free and easy, and the New Zealand girls quiet and dignified, but very friendly. The South African girls reminded us of the Southerners from the United States. The English were much harder to approach. The unrestricted rules left us pretty well able to please ourselves and our individual fancies.

In company of two New Zealand Nursing Sisters, we explored the many woodland roads that seemed to run in all directions, or gathered green pine cones. In the evening we tossed these into the open fire and their burning filled the whole room with perfume.

Not far from the hospital was a British encampment. One evening Lady Gifford invited several of us to go with her to a concert to be given by an English entertaining troupe for the soliders. We enjoyed a very fine soprano soloist, as well as an amusing farce. It was the community singing of the army and the old familiar songs that we enjoyed the most.

Near the end of the week, Lady Seymour decided to take us all on a route march. Take it from me, the English women are the best walkers in the whole world.

Our colds had cleared up, and I had regained my voice, so we felt that we were fit for a couple of miles walking. With Lady Seymour and Mouski the dog leading the way with long, graceful strides, we set out. Not far down the road from the hospital we came to the Blue Cross Hospital, the horses standing in rows of stalls; roans, bays, black and chestnut, no doubt wondering what it was all about. One beautiful bay stretched out his neck to be patted, giving me a feeling of guilt that I did not have some sugar or an apple to offer him. Like the soliders, some of them had horrible skin wounds. We wondered if, when they were once more fit, they would be sent back within range of the guns, for whatever purpose that they were used. It did seem a shame.

From the Blue Cross Hospital, Lady Seymour took a pathway leading off the main road, over fields that reminded me of Canada. Through privet hedges we followed our leader, until we came in sight of a small village. Long before this the colonials were bringing up the rear, at a distance of some rods. We were glad to find that, before our arrival, preparations had been made ahead at a small restaurant for afternoon tea. We had walked a distance of five miles. It seemed ten.

It was late in the afternoon when we started our return trip home. This time we took the main highway route that led directly past the hospital. After about three miles, six of us asked permission to be allowed to sit down and wait for a passing transport. There we sat for over an hour, and the sun went down. We were beginning to think that we would have to start walking, or be there for the night, when we heard the screech of steel wheels on the pavement in the distance. Stretching arm in arm across the road in a line, we hailed the driver of the huge vehicle. Never before was I so thankful for a ride, even though the noise was deafening and the ride uncomfortable, sitting as we were on the floor of the truck. As we reached the stone pillars leading into the hospital grounds, we passed lady Seymour with her companions, swinging along as if they were on the first lap, not the last, of a ten mile route march. We were thankful to crawl into bed and rest, glad too, that with the morrow we could once more be back in our own camp and on duty.

On our arrival at No. 3 Stationary, we were surprised to hear that we were due for another move. We were to go up nearer the front line in preparation for the winter. Personally, I was weary of this eternal moving. Breaking up hospital involved so much shifting around. Each time, we were sent to a hotel or attached to one of the other hospitals, until our own new hospital was made ready for us. Once more we supervised the packing of our ward supplies and the evacuation of all patients. Most of those able to be moved were sent to England. As I stood at the door of our tent and watched the large marquees flattened to the ground, and rolled into neat bundles, I had a premonition that it was the last time I would watch my home of so many months, being taken down and packed away. Soon the whole campground had the appearance of desolation. It gave me a very homesick sensation.

Chapter Ten; Editor's Notes

1) Captain Gustav Adolf Khuring was a graduate of the University of Toronto, 1898-1901. He served as a Chaplain with the No.3 CSH at Lemnos from August 1915 and moved with the unit to France. Khuring stayed in France until December 1916 when he was moved to England. He resigned from the Services in April 1917.

Chapter Eleven

Etaples Once More

Along with four other Sisters, Sister Willett and I were attached to No. 7 Canadian Stationary Hospital at Etaples. Where No. 3 was to be located, we had no idea. I was glad it was to No. 7 Canadian Stationary that we were being sent, as this hospital and staff had been our travelling companions as far as Alexandria, Egypt in 1915. On our arrival I was told that I was to go on duty, as a special with a heart case, regardless of the fact that we had been up early and travelling all day. I found my patient in Sister Allan's marquee. I had worked with Sister Allan when I had been Supervisor at No. 1 Canadian General Hospital. She greeted me with an amused smile on her face when I asked for my night orders.

I do not think that you will have a very strenuous night," she remarked and proceeded to give me a report of the history of the case.

The Medical Officer was very young and a new arrival of only a few days. This was his first time on duty on the wards. My case was a shell shock, who had been admitted with an erratic heart action (Who wouldn't have?). The Captain had become alarmed and demanded a special nurse on duty at once, unsettling himself and the patient at the time. Sister Allan just laughed.

"Just give the boy time. After he has run into a hundred of these cases he will not be asking for specials." This meant a shortage of nurses on the wards. I happened along at just the right time as an extra.

I was really sorry for the patient's state of mind. I rather think that he had come to the conclusion that it was up to him to pass away, when so much fuss had been made. He looked up with a tragic expression and asked if I thought that he would live through the night until morning. I sat down and talked quietly with him for some time, then told him to go to sleep and forget about himself, and that I would sit by his side and see he came safely through. Finally I had eased his fears and he fell into a sound sleep. When he wakened at daybreak, he looked up and smiled, "Well, Sister no chance of pushing daisies this morning?" The frightened expression had left his face. Several days later he waved a cheery goodbye, as he left for England and home.

No. 7 Canadian Stationary Hospital was part of the new wooden hut hospital city. When I had been on duty in 1915, in Etaples, the hills now covered with wooden huts had been a city of canvas marquees. More and more the war and all branches of it seemed to have settled down into a systematic business, complete with conveniences. No more were candles used as a lighting system. These had been replaced by electricity. In the Nursing Sisters' quarters were several bath houses. Galvanized iron tubs had been installed, and there was an abundance of steaming hot water, both day and night. About the only inconvenience we had to suffer was having some distance to walk between the sleeping huts and the bath houses, in our bedroom slippers and dressing gowns. This, however, was a considerable improvement on Lemnos Island, when our weekly bath meant a trip up the mountains to the hot springs. So we tried to be thankful when, at 6:30 a.m., we clenched our teeth to still the chattering, and ran for the bathhouse.

In the mess hut a youth with a mop of fair hair served our meals. Often he succeeded in calling down the wrath of many of the Nursing Sisters on his defenseless head, while crimson blushes played all over his sensitive face. Years later, in Canada, the union of churches was being thrashed out, my own church going through a period of stress and strain with many dissenters. I sat in a pew and watched the same abused orderly mount the steps to the platform and, from his pulpit, deliver an eloquent sermon on the text, "His house shall be called desolate." Mentally I was patting him on the back, but all the while I was seeing him passing out gray army mugs and gray granite plates.

There were many things this ruthless war had taught me: How little it mattered what religion we belonged to; whether the soldier be the master or the servant; if he brought honour to his regiment and himself he was our hero without prejudice. It mattered little whether the dying boy was comforted by a Protestant or a Roman Catholic. We were united in one great effort, victory for our army, with which we hoped would come peace for all time.

The German prison camp lay just west of the hospital. Early in 1915 it had been very small, now it seemed filled to overflowing. That reminds me of a very embarrassing position my ward sister and I were placed in. Being only loaned to No. 7 Hospital for a short time, I was placed on a ward as an assistant.

One morning we were interrupted in our work by the arrival of a British Tommy who pushed two husky prisoners inside the door while he stood on guard outside. Sister Abernathy and I held a consultation between ourselves, before we approached the prisoners, as to what we would do about the whole affair. We wondered what was wrong with them, and why we had been burdened with them. I suggested that, since they both looked so healthy, rheumatism might be a good guess. It was the first malady that popped into my head. Not being able to speak German, the sister followed the habit many people have of speaking to a foreigner in a loud tone of voice, as if his hearing might be impaired, because he can not speak our own language.

"What is the matter with you, have you rheumatism?", she asked the first man.

"Ya" he answered. She asked the second, "Ya, ya" he answered with a nod of his black head.

She turned to me with a resigned air. "I guess there is nothing for it but to put them to bed." With the help of the orderly, the two German prisoners were soon resting peacefully in two of our nice clean beds.

Possibly half an hour later a sergeant came to the door, took a look inside the hut and, not seeing any sign of the prisoners, turned with alarm to Sister Abernathy, asking her what she had done with the two "Boshies" he had sent over.

"Put them to bed" she replied. "What did you expect us to do, give them afternoon tea?" Indignation was in every syllable she uttered.

For a moment he just stood there, looking at her, then he burst out laughing.

"Good God, woman I sent them over to scrub your floors."

We presented them each with a pail of hot water and a scrub brush, while the men in the ward simply howled with laughter, in which the two prisoners joined. As if to add insult to injury we discovered that they could both speak perfect English, having lived in Canada for some years.

Influenza in the Unit

The days were growing shorter and colder. Pneumonia patients who required careful nursing were being admitted every day. An epidemic of a virulent 'flu' had broken out. Many of the Sisters were laid off duty. Just before Christmas I became ill with the same virus. When well enough I was invalided to England and admitted to the St. George Hospital for sick Nursing Sisters. Situated almost at the back of Buckingham Palace, this improvised little hospital had been a boys' private school in peacetime. From the general appearance of the building it might be hundreds of years old. The small windows were very deep set. The woodwork was dark and scarred from age, and perhaps the abuse it had received from its former inmates. The ceiling in my private room was low and sloping, the floors surprisingly rough and uneven. However, it was scrupulously clean, and bright fires were kept burning day and night in the small open grate fireplaces in each room.

Being fortunate in having my own room, I was very quiet, and received the very best of attention from the Nursing Sister in charge. When I recovered and was well enough to sit up, I was allowed to go to the tiny sitting room, along with the other convalescing patients, most of whom had been victims of the influenza. I found them all very interesting. Several of the sisters had seen service in India, and had many interesting stories to relate. There were one or two who had received wounds from pieces of flying shrapnel during bombing raids. Perhaps the one that I felt the most sorry for was the small English Nursing Sister, who had been on duty on the *Anglia* hospital ship. It had been torpedoed in the English Channel by a German submarine that was no respecter of the Red Cross hospital ships. She was recovering from shock, and a nervous breakdown. She did not seem to be able to forget the horror of it all for even one hour. She had been on duty on an upper deck with sixty-five stretcher cases, practically all old country boys, in high spirits at the prospects of being so close to home, and seeing their people once more. One boy had complained of a headache, and the sister had turned to the medicine cupboard on the deck's wall to get some aspirin. Suddenly there was a terrific noise, as of a blow. With no warning, or realization of what had happened, she found herself clinging fast to a ladder fastened to the wall, with water swirling all around her knees. She looked around for her patients, but they were

Ravages of Influenza

Spreading Everywhere.

Safeguard yourself by using

MILTON

MILTON will effectively prevent the infection of Influenza. You cannot catch Influenza if you use MILTON according to instructions. It's the real safeguard.

This is a strong statement, but it is absolutely true.

Influenza is a germ disease—a catching infection. Germs cannot exist where MILTON is present. If used as a mouth wash and nasal spray morning and night (about two minutes' attention and it does not smart) you will be immune.

MILTON, in proportion of half a teaspoonful to a glass of tepid water, used three times a day (snuffed up the nose or used with an ordinary spray and also as a gargle) will be found to work like a charm.

Get a 1/3 or 2/6 bottle of MILTON from your dealer to-day.

It makes an effective barrage through which the enemy cannot penetrate.

MILTON is sold in 1/3 & 2/6 bottles

To be obtained from all Dealers.

Milton Manufacturing Co., Ltd., 125, Bunhill Row, London, E.C.1, and 64, Wellington St., Glasgow

**Don't Sneeze—
Use Milton.**

Milton is the best preventive against Colds in the Head, Catarrh and similar Winter complaints.

Ad for Ravages of Influenza.

all gone, swept overboard with the rush of water. She clung to the ladder with all her strength, but could never remember how or when she had been rescued by one of the lifeboats. It was little wonder that, after such an experience, she could find no peace of mind, awake or asleep.

One afternoon I opened my eyes to find Sister Willett, with an armful of roses, standing by my bedside. I rubbed my eyes to make sure that she was real, then almost wept for joy. After I had written to her that it would be some time before I would be able to return to active service, she had decided to apply for transport duty to Canada, which would give her three weeks home leave. She had hoped that I would be nearly enough recovered to accompany her by getting sick leave. For once fate stepped in and separated us. The following night she sailed for home.

I was given sick leave when I was discharged, and this I spent with relatives who lived in "Chambers" in the Inner Temple of the law courts on Kings Bench Walk, in the very heart of old London. As I climbed the very steep steps to the top of the building I felt as if I must be dreaming. I had taken a taxi to the doorway leading from the Strand to the Inner Temple Court yard, and, once inside, turned to the right, and passed under an ancient archway, forming the vestibule of a small Anglican church. I found myself in the Inner Court, where I came face to face with a small company of older men (nicknamed England's Last Hope) training for guard duty. They were doing the goose step to the orders of a red-faced sergeant. They were so old and so intent on what they were doing, that I stood to watch them, until the sergeant gave me a withering look, and one old fellow waved his hat at me.

By that time I was feeling rather self-conscious and hurried across the yard to No. 6 Kings Bench Walk, one of a row of solid-looking stone buildings. I entered a very narrow doorway and proceeded to climb the steep stairway. On the first landing, on the door plate I noted the name of Lord Northcliffe. Apparently the first two or three stories were given over to different law offices. There seemed to be so many steps it was like climbing the spiral stairway to Napoleon's Monument.

The top floor was given over to 'Chambers' (apartments) for anyone connected with the law courts. Here my cousin lived with her Barrister husband, entitled to live within the courts. She was waiting for me in her charming livingroom. The floors were covered wall to wall with soft gray carpet, the pile making it feel like velvet under your feet. On the plain white walls hung many black and white etchings. At the wide front windows, overlooking the Court below, hung rich mulberry drapes. A very wide, gray marble fireplace was at one end of the room, and over the fireplace hung a large, framed chippendale mirror. While we sat and chatted she told me the history of the Inner Court Temple. It dated back to the time of Charles I. In a state of intoxication he was persuaded to sign papers exempting the Chambers of the Inner Court from paying rent. Although the tenants were expected to pay an honorary fee, this was not compulsory. Also, the tenants must in some way be connected with the law courts.

The bedroom that I occupied was a tiny room with a slanting ceiling and one small hinged window. It was the more interesting when I was told that it was the room occupied by Charles Dickens, when he transposed Shakespeare's plays to prose. I could almost feel the spirit of those old golden ages about the whole place, even to the closing of the gate leading out into the Strand, at midnight. If you tarried outside later than that, you were obliged to lift the huge knocker of the hobnailed door leading onto the street and rap. A very small old man made his appearance, first by taking a look at you through the tiny window in the door. He would let you in with a cheery "Good night Miss", and you would hear the door close behind you, as he once more retreated to his watch-room close by. Outside of the door, leading to the Inner Court on the Strand, the ceremony of presenting the keys to the city to the Lord Mayor took place once a year.

The Inner Temple is completely surrounded by the law courts. The names of the streets running in all directions are very familiar to most of us who have read Charles Dickens' books. Chancery Lane, Fleet Street and the Strand border the famous law court buildings. My cousin had a treasure store of interesting stories to tell. For instance I learned, that Charles Dickens sat before the fireplace in my cousin's living room with his friend Charles Lamb, and read to him many of his manuscripts.

Mrs. Loughborough Ball, charming and intelligent, was born in Owen Sound, Ontario, where she lived until she married her Barrister husband, who had taken her back to England with him as a bride. She was still very loyal to Canada, and not content to sit with her hands folded, while our men were at war. Along with her sister Helen, and

Mrs. Christopher Eaton from Owen Sound, they opened the Grey Rooms in London for Canadian soldiers. There the boys found a home away from home in many ways. They could go there for information regarding trains and buses. They could sit and read the Canadian papers, or have afternoon tea, all provided free. Mrs. Ball also entered the V.A.D. service, stationed at Charing Cross depot, where she conducted an information bureau, directing soldiers from the colonies and West Indies what buses to take or changes to make, the shortest route to Scotland or Ireland, where to find the soup canteen, etc. Small and dainty, she was very dynamic. What a keen sense of direction and knowledge of London, England she must have possessed. Twice a week she invited to her home for dinner at least two soldiers, sometimes Officers, sometimes non-commissioned officers. But most often two privates, if they appealed to her as being very lonely.

Chapter Eleven; Editor's Notes

1) The Number Seven Canadian Stationary Hospital (Dalhousie) served in England from January to June 1916. It was transferred to Le Havre, France in June 1916 and was moved several times in 1916-1919. Its locations in France were; Harfleur, Arques, Etaples, Rouen and Camiers. It returned to England in March 1919.

2) Lord Alfred Northcliffe (1865-1922) was Britain's most influential newspaper magnate. His publications were popular and he used his power and connections to influence the war effort.

Chapter Twelve

I Become Engaged to an Army Officer

While recuperating at my cousin's home in the Inner Temple, mail forwarded to me brought a letter from Lieutenant Simmie, with the information that he was on sick leave in Manchester, England. I was not surprised when he came to see me. Both on army sick leave, we spent the time sightseeing Westminster Abbey with all its magnificent architecture, antique gems and ancient historical information. We visited St. Paul's Cathedral with its whispering gallery, its boys' choir with voices so sweet and clear, their music would almost break one's heart. We saw the Parliament Buildings, even the Inner Temple where I was staying, with its Law Courts and Coptic Church. We went outside of the city to small, quaint villages, with thatched cottages.

We attended many fine plays, saw "Choo Chin Chow" at his Majesty's theatre, where it had been running for two years. We attended several light operas; "Tonight's the Night", where I was moved to tears when I remembered my little Private Foster at No. 3 Canadian Stationary Hospital at Boulogne. He had been one of the dancers in the show when he enlisted. Several times we attended musicals at Albert Hall, where we heard the famous contralto, Clara Butt. We dined at the Trocadero, where I ran into several of my old Australian and New Zealand nursing sisters. We also had dinner at Claridges, where Kings, Queens and many famous celebrities had been guests in the past. It was all marvellous for two young people who had just become engaged.

When I reported for duty once more the examining officer decided I was still not fit for active duty. Remembering that I had served in the East, he suggested home leave. At that time a hundred or more Canadian soldiers were being sent back to Canadian hospitals, and would leave in four days time. I was appointed Nursing Sister in charge with Captain Bell (Ohio, U.S.A.) in charge. Captain Bell had been with us on staff while we were at the Dardanelles. I looked forward to the crossing with pleasure. As it turned out Captain Bell proved to be allergic to the sea, and took to his bed. I carried on with little or nothing to do, other than a few minor dressings, adjusting bandages etc. It was not a difficult task. Lieutenant Simmie, still on sick leave, applied for home leave. One cold wintry day in February, 1917 we sailed from Liverpool on the *Magnetawan*, a small troop ship, the smallest one that I had ever travelled on. But I was thrilled to be on my way home, with a three week leave.

It was not a smooth crossing; we ran into several snow storms, and had to zig-zag to avoid the German submarine, the *Black Raider*, that we learned was on our trail. This took us on a sort of a wild goose chase. Only by following the daily bulletin board would we have any idea as to our route. Thanks to the snow storm our boat was almost invisible most of the time. When we reached St. John, New Brunswick, I was so happy I could have kissed the very ground, snow and all. When we boarded our long Canadian train coach, we knew that we were really home. We had one day's stay in Montreal before we left for Toronto. The only unpleasant time was when some well wishing visitor gave two of my patients too much to drink. This time I was allergic, and Captain Bell took over completely.

Home Again

Toronto Union Station was a happy place that February day in 1917, with friends of the returning soldiers waiting to give the wounded a welcome home. Laughter and tears were mingled. A band was playing; happy confusion prevailed. The last boy off the train seemed to be all alone. I took his kit as we walked toward the waiting room, and as we walked we talked. He was very depressed. Being from Northern Ontario, and having been an ardent hockey player, he was thoroughly despising the crutches he was using to replace his amputated limb. Coming home to Canada seemed to emphasize what it really meant to be handicapped. I was sincerely wishing him luck. As I said goodbye, I almost added the familiar farewell used in France: "Up the line with the best of luck".

It was so good, so good to be home. My own home village welcomed me with open arms. Owen Sound followed with a civic reception. I was presented with an address by the Mayor of the town, Mr. R.D. Little. A school girl, representing all the schools in town, presented me with an armful of roses. A boy soloist from Ryerson School sang

Lieutenant Simmie.

Captain Simmie, his new wife, Kate Wilson, and two others in Kansas City.

my favorite CooCoo song, his lovely, clear, boyish voice so well suited to the song. Mrs. Andrew Haye, proclaiming me a Real Daughter of
the Empire, pinned the emblem on my uniform, and made me a life
member of the Daughters of the Empire. The Superintendent of my
own General and Marine Hospital and my training school, and Miss
Mary Sim presented me with a bouquet of flowers and she read an
address, shaking as if she might have been facing a firing squad.

When my three weeks were expired, I reported once more for duty
in Ottawa. I was not surprised when I stepped off the train, to find my
fiance waiting for me on the platform. His medical board had found
him unfit for future active service. We had planned both to return to
duty for the duration. He was disappointed and furious, but there was
little that he could do about it. Having won the Military Cross at the
Battle of Courcelette he had hoped to go back and see the finish of the
war. However, at Headquarters they had offered to send him to the
United States in charge of the British-Canadian Recruiting Mission.
Under these circumstances, we decided that I would get my discharge
and go with him.

In order to get my discharge from the army I had to go to
Headquarters. This I did, and, owing to the fact I had done the full
Dardanelles campaign and was recovering from an attack of influenza
with complications, I had no difficulty in getting my discharge.

Major T. Thompson, one of our Padres while we were at the
Dardanelles, had been invalided back to his home in Ottawa. As with
so many wartime marriages, we were married very quietly at Major
Thompson's home. Not long after this my husband's promotion to the
rank of Captain came through, and we were sent to Kansas City,
Missouri, a very interesting place. It looked as if at one time it might
have been a group of bluffs, most of them cone-shaped. In the planning
the bluffs were left, and the city built up around them, especially on the
Missouri side. The Mississippi River, one of the dirtiest and muddiest
rivers that I had ever seen, ran directly through the heart of the city,
dividing Kansas City, Missouri from Kansas City, Kansas. When my
husband, with a twinkle in his eye, informed me that the Mississippi
was the source of the city's water supply, I decided then and there to go
on bottled mineral water for the duration.

The British-Canadian Recruiting Mission was located on Main

Street, Kansas City, Missouri. It was a very beautiful residential area, known then as the Sun Set district, a very exclusive and wealthy part of the city. There were parks, including the then famous Swope Park as well as Churches of every denomination, and attractive Municipal buildings. Evidently money had not been taken into consideration in the planning of either the exterior or interior of these buildings.

A British-Canadian Recruiting Mission seemed like a very dull undertaking after active duty overseas. To go recruiting men in another country, one that they had used as their way of escape, was almost like bringing an enemy into their territory. Under Brigadier General White, these Missions were being established. Captain Simmie was to have charge of the depot at 901 Main St., Kansas City, Mo. Canada was sending seasoned officers who had seen active service and had been invalided back home, disabled for further duty in the field. They were assisted by returned disabled men. Their work was to recruit, with the assistance of the managers and staff of the manufacturing firms, men who had crossed over into the United States to avoid entering the war.

There were four states to cover. Almost every night Captain Simmie was speaking in some town or city. It was a dangerous job. Many of the men they were trying to reach were slackers. For the first time in my life I was terrified. Never once had fear crossed my mind while I was overseas and on active service. I almost dreaded to read the daily papers because there seemed to be so much crime afoot. I feared mostly for my husband. The men of the Recruiting Mission were not exactly popular, especially in the factory districts, where a greater part of the work was done. Lists of names were compiled by the different firms, and from these the military worked.

The people of Kansas City gave us a very warm welcome, and we made many friends. There were times when I was amazed and surprised at how little was known about Canada or its history. I was amused to be asked by a school teacher who the Canadians really originated from. I almost said "Mohawks", but on second thought I feared she might take me seriously.

I remembered that before leaving France we had waited for word that the United States had joined forces with us, as we felt that sooner or later they would. President Wilson's notes had become a joke; we knew that they would have to make up their minds sooner or later. Just before we left for Kansas City, the United States had declared war on Germany. Months passed, reminding me of Canada in the first stages of the war. Finally the Americans crossed over into France. One morning, while travelling on a street car, a woman sat beside me, reading a newspaper carrying the headlines "Casualties: Thirteen Dead". She turned to me, knowing that I was a Canadian.

"Well, the war will soon be over, now that our boys are in the field," she said. I drew out of my shopping bag the English copy of the London Daily Mail I had received the day before. I opened it and showed it to her. Page after page listed the casualties of our different forces.

These are our casualties for one day, and these are the men who will be known as those who won the war, when it is won. They are the men who stepped in and held trenches and lines, and are still holding them."

She looked shocked and could scarcely believe it, but there was the evidence. She was utterly speechless.

Chapter Thirteen

The Armistice

On November 11th, 1918, the war was ended, the war to end all wars. I was so happy that it was all over, and we could all go home.

An editorial from the Advocate, a London, Ontario magazine at the time the war was ended, gives a good idea of the reaction of a city, as well as many smaller places throughout the country in Canada, to the Armistice. I would like to add this to my story:

"The Armistice - We were wakened by the clanging of bells. Bedroom doors were opened and one voice called to another down the corridor. In a moment the factory whistles began. In the sound of the bells there was a joyous vibrancy; the whistles were tooting with a holiday quality hitherto unknown in them. There could be only one meaning to such concatenation; the war was over. The next moment the shrill voices of the newsboys came steadily nearer. I grabbed a "quarter" and flew down stairs, in bare feet and night gown. I was out on the porch whose floor was white with frost. "War Extra"- It was the familiar weary old cry become habit, but followed by a new one, "Armistice Declared!" All the way up the street the lights were going on in houses and shining through open doors. A lad on a bicycle half tumbled off at our step. "War extra, Lady?" I caught the sheet as he handed it to me, and ran upstairs, at whose top in the ghastly light of a single bulb, with dishevelled hair and open dressing gown, stood the other two females in the household, peering eagerly into the gloom below from which I was emerging, and called excitedly, "Is it really true, is the war over?" We gathered in a bedroom and I tried to read the brief paragraphs set in heavy type. Our family had odd ways of expressing extreme joy, and mine was to weep uncontrollably. I broke down into hysterical sobbing, and handed the paper to Rene, who... was much less ridiculous over it."

Yes it was true, the great news which the world had been longing for, through cruel days that had dragged on so long that it seemed as though the sickening slaughter in Europe-where so many of our boys were had gone on since the beginning of time, and would go on to the end of it.

We opened the windows and stuck our heads out. At about four in the morning the stars hung clear in the luminous night sky. Silence and Majesty above, and below, on the keen frosty air, was borne converging toward the heart of the city, a rising murmur, punctuated by sharp staccato noises, the honk of motor cars, the click of hurrying feet, voices shouting. Presently the flare of a light above the dense business section. Next morning, we heard that an over-exuberant part of the crowd, surging about the news bulletins, had suddenly rushed off and started bonfires with old chairs, old tables, anything that would burn, and with such success that the flames threatened to melt the network of wire at a main crossing, so that it was necessary to call the fire-brigade. Also, it was told that the jam of people, milling about until morning, and feeling the need of some expression, had turned the occasion into a sort of Mardi Gras. Ticklers were produced as if by magic, talcum powder was thrown about, tin cans dragged at the rear of automobiles, small whistles and horns helping to make bedlam - All the old tricks, usually more artificially produced for bygone, carefree "Old Boys" reunions.

Meanwhile, away out in the great dome of the night where farm houses slept in darkness, and the scattered night lights of small towns and villages twinkled like tiny constellations on the face of the dim silent earth, the glad tidings were beginning to trickle through, telephones rang and the surge of joy threaded, alas, with so much sorrow - moved on.

Joy, sorrow and a touch of comedy, too - but people did not laugh then, only afterwards. Letters came, telling me of how the news was received in one small village, the one I call home. Perhaps something similar had been told of many others. Among the first in our small town, Chatsworth, Ontario, near Owen Sound, to hear the shrill call of the telephone was a kindly maiden lady who lived across the street from the Presbyterian church. Her first thought was to let everyone know, and, under the urge, the next was to fly across the street and tug vigorously at the church bell rope. The louder, the faster the bell rang, the better satisfied she was. Everyone would be sure to be up and out because from time immemorial the Presbyterian bell had been the village fire alarm. As a matter of fact, before five minutes the whole population, alarmed by the energetic and protracted ringing, was outdoors in coats and bedroom slippers, anxiously scanning the roof tops for signs of an angry glare... Then far away sounds of whistles in the nearest town came over the hills. Other telephones began ringing and the joyful word passed from lip to lip.

The villagers, like the citizens of larger places, must also find expression. Down the street every house was alight. Someone suggested (appropriately enough, surely) that something religious was in order, so a number who could sing - or make a pretense at it-gathered at a corner of one of the streets and sang "O God our help in Ages Past". Meanwhile a crowd of different ideals had collected at the hotel corner, where, from an undertakers' parlor nearby, a rough box was presently brought forth with the letters in black vividly painted along the side, "To Hell with the Kaiser". In the twinkling of an eye a bonfire roared in the middle of the street, and to make the symbolism more graphic, the rough box was hoisted on the top, where, being very dry, it soon blazed merrily. . the citizens who had thought of speeches put on their stunt, and some very good ones were delivered from the local portico, albeit a speaker or two, whose idea of a celebration could not ignore the time honoured custom became more loquacious than eloquent. Perhaps the funniest of all was that, beyond the bonfire, beyond the singers singing devoutly, never budging from the Post Office steps, stood the postmaster, one of the quietest and least demonstrative of Scots, solemnly and continuously firing off a shotgun into the air. Joy! Joy! Joy!

A strange delirium, that could make some weep for relief, and others faint, and some go foolishly berserk, and the quietest and dourest of men stand firing shots into the air. A delirium revealing tension of the strain now broken - the unnaturalness and cruelty of a condition that never should have been - yet, in little rooms all over the lands - in cities, villages and farms - mothers, sisters and sweethearts were silently weeping for those who would not come back "When the boys come marching"; lads who, in the flower of strength of their manhood, had fallen in France and Flanders, and were sleeping beneath the poppies and little white crosses in an alien land."

In our little village, and almost every village of its size there stands a monument. Ours is a simple, dignified shaft of granite with a pall indicated in hard stone, its fold drawn back to reveal a long list of names - names of lads of the village and surrounding countryside, whom we all knew; wholesome, cheery lads who hated no one, but who marched away with high hearts to fight, as they thought, in the war to end wars. "The war that was to end wars"- the irony of it - the cruel irony of it, in the lurid light of day! Oh God, how long shall these things be?

I have told my story, tried to keep it simple. Now I will dismiss my visions with the many happy memories of the past. There may be some old veteran who, reading this, will remember the mountains and valleys of the little Island of Lemnos in the Aegean Sea. The blue waters of the Mediterranean, the glorious Egyptian nights with the indigo blue skies, the tinkle of an anklet on an Egyptian maiden as she passes by, balancing her tray of treasures on the top of her head. He may see, in memory, the gay stalls of Cairo's bazaars, the stern silent pryamids, the Sphinx with the mutilated nose; the beautiful gardens of the Grande Palace of Versailles; the scarlet poppies and blue cornflowers growing in the fields of wheat; hear the marching of feet, hear in the valley below the bray of a donkey, the echo of the bugler's horn on the hillside as they sound "*Lights out.*"

Nursing Roll of Honour
Overseas, 1914-1918

Baker, Margaret Elisa, N/S; Toronto, Ontario; died of disease May 30th, 1919; buried Ayr, Scotland; Age 45.

Baker, Miriam Eastman, N/S, No. 15 CGH; Winnipeg, Manitoba; died of disease October 17th, 1918; buried Cliveden War Cemetery, Taplow, U.K.; Age 32.

Baldwin, Dorothy Mary Yarwood, N/S, No. 3 CSH; Toronto, Ontario; killed in an enemy air raid at Doullens, France, May 30th, 1918; buried Bagneux, France. Age 27.

Campbell, Christina, N/S; Victoria, British Columbia; drowned when the HS Llandovery Castle was sunk by a German U-Boat, June 27th, 1918; commemorated on the Halifax Memorial; Age 45.

Dagg, Ainslie St.Clair, N/S, No.15 CGH; died of disease November 29th, 1918; buried Cliveden War Cemetery, Taplow, U.K.; Age 26.

Davis, Lena Alva, N/S, No. 4 CGH; Bramsville, Ontario; died of disease February 21st, 1918; buried Sherborne, Hampshire, U.K.; Age 33.

Douglas, Carola Josephine, N/S; Toronto, Ontario; drowned when the HS Llandovery Castle was sunk by a German U-Boat, June 27th, 1918; commemorated on the Halifax Memorial. Age 31.

Dussault, Alexina, N/S; Montreal, Quebec; drowned when the HS Llandovery Castle was sunk by a German U-Boat, June 27th, 1918; commemorated on the Halifax Memorial; Age 36.

Follette, Minnie Asenath, N/S; Wards Brook, Nova Scotia; drowned when the HS Llandovery Castle was sunk by a German U-Boat, June 27th, 1918; commemorated on the Halifax Memorial; Age 34.

Forneri, Agnes Florien, N/S, No. 8 CGH; Belleville, Ontario; died of disease April 24th, 1918; buried Bramshott, Hampshire, U.K.; Age 39. Her brother David was killed in France on March 1st, 1917.

Fortescue, Margaret Jane, N/S; York Factory; drowned when the HS Llandovery Castle was sunk by a German U-Boat, June 27th, 1918; commemorated on the Halifax Memorial; Age 40.

Fraser, Margaret Marjory, Matron; New Glasgow, Nova Scotia; drowned when the HS Llandovery Castle was sunk by a German U-Boat, June 27th, 1918; commemorated on the Halifax Memorial; Age 34.

Gallaher, Minnie Katherine, N/S; Pittsburg, Ontario; drowned when the HS Llandovery Castle was sunk by a German U-Boat, June 27th, 1918; commemorated on the Halifax Memorial; Age 38.

Garbutt, Sarah Ellen, N/S, Ontario Military Hospital; Oshawa, Ontario; died of disease August 20th, 1917; buried Brookwood, Surrey, England; Age 42.

Green, Matilda Ethel, N/S, No.7 CGH; Virden, Manitoba; died of pneumonia October 9th, 1918; buried Etaples, France. Age 32.

Hennan, Victoria Belle, N/S, No.9 CGH; Poland, Manitoba; died of disease October 23rd, 1918; buried Shorncliffe, Kent, England. Age 32.

Jaggard, Jessie Brown, Matron, No.3 CSH; King's County, Nova Scotia; died of dysentery, September 25th, 1915; buried Portiannos, Lemnos, Greece. Age 44.

Jenner, Lenna Mae, N/S; Brookfield, Nova Scotia; died of disease December 12th, 1918; buried Brookwood, Surrey, England; Age 29.

Kealy, Ida Lillian, N/S, No.1 CGH; Edmonton, Alberta; died of pneumonia March 12th, 1918; buried Bramshott, Hampshire, England. Age 39.

King, Jessie Nelson, N/S, No.1 CGH; died of disease April 4th, 1919; Victoria, British Columbia; buried Terlincthun, France. Age 27.

Lowe, Margaret, N/S, No.1 CGH; Binscarth, Manitoba; died of wounds received in an enemy air raid at Etaples, May 28th, 1918; buried Etaples, France. Age 32.

McDiarmid, Jessie Mabel, N/S, No.5 CGH; Black's Corners, Ontario; drowned when the HS Llandovery Castle was sunk by a German U-Boat, June 27th, 1918; commemorated on the Halifax, Memorial. Age 38.

MacDonald, Katherine Maude, N/S, No.1 CGH; Brantford, Ontario; killed in a enemy air raid at Etaples, May 19th, 1918; buried Etaples, France. Age 31.

McIntosh, Rebecca, N/S, No.9 CGH; Truro, Nova Scotia; died of pneumonia March 7th, 1919; buried Bodelwyddan, Wales. Age 25.

McKay, EvelynVerrall, N/S. No.3 CGH; Galt, Ontario; died of disease November 4th, 1918. Age 27.

McKenzie, Mary Agnes, N/S; Toronto, Ontario; drowned when the HS Llandovery Castle was sunk by a German U-Boat, June 27th, 1918; commemorated on the Halifax Memorial. Age 40.

McLean, Rena Maude, N/S; Souris, Prince Edward Island; drowned when the HS Llandovery Castle was sunk by a German U-Boat, June 27th, 1918; commemorated on the Halifax Memorial. Age 39.

MacPherson, Agnes, N/S, No.3 CSH; Brandon, Manitoba; killed in a enemy air raid at Doullens, France, May 30th, 1918; buried Bagneux, France. Age 27.

Mellett, Henrietta, N/S, No.15 CGH; London, Ontario; drowned when the SS Leinster was sunk by a German submarine, October 10th, 1918; buried Dublin, Eire. Age 39.

Munroe, Mary Frances Elizabeth, N/S, No.3 CSH; Wardsville, Ontario; died of dysentery, Limnos, 1915; buried Portannos, Greece. Age 49.

Pringle, Eden Lyal, N/S, No.3 CSH; Vancouver, British Columbia; killed in a enemy air raid at Doullens, France, May 30th, 1918; buried Bagneux, France. Age 25.

Ross, Ada Janet, N/S, No.1 CGH; Toronto, Ontario; died of disease July 12th, 1918; buried Buxton, Derbyshire, England. Age 50.

Sampson, Mary Belle, N/S; Duntroon, Ontario; drowned when the HS Llandovery Castle was sunk by a German U-Boat, June 27th, 1918; commemorated on the Halifax Memorial. Age 28.

Sare, Gladys Irene, N/S; Montreal, Quebec; drowned when the HS Llandovery Castle was sunk by a German U-Boat, June 27th, 1918; commemorated on the Halifax Memorial. Age 29. Her brother, Harry, was killed at Vimy Ridge.

Sparks, Etta, N/S, No.7 CGH; Britannia, Ontario; died of disease August 20th, 1917; buried Brighton, Sussex, England. Age 38.

Stamers, Anna Irene, N/S, St.John, New Brunswick; drowned when the HS Llandovery Castle was sunk by a German U-Boat, June 27th, 1918; commemorated on the Halifax Memorial. Age 30.

Templeman, Jean, N/S; Ottawa, Ontario; drowned when the HS Llandovery Castle was sunk by a German U-Boat, June 27th, 1918; commemorated on the Halifax Memorial. Age 33.

Tupper, Addie Allen, N/S. No.2 CGH; Yarmouth, Nova Scotia; died of disease December 9th, 1916; buried Hillingdon, Middlesex, England. Age 46.

Wake, Gladys Mary Maude, N/S, No.1 CGH; Esquimalt, British Columbia; died of wounds received in an enemy air raid at Etaples, May 21st, 1918; buried Etaples, France. Age 34.

Whitely, Anna Elizabeth, N/S, No.10 CSH; Manvers, Ontario; died of disease April 24th, 1918; buried Wimereux, France. Age 36.

Katharine Mildred Wilson

(1887-1984)

Katharine Mildred Wilson was born in Chatsworth, Ontario, October 15th, 1887, of United Empire Loyalist stock. She was brought up in a strict Scotch Presbyterian household. The family was raised in a cultured environment where education, music and religion played a major role. All six Wilson children played musical instruments. Of course, true to their Scotch Presbyterian beliefs, there was no liquor or dancing in the house. Such entertainments were forbidden. Life was hard in the 1890s and medical knowledge inadequate to cope with the epidemics that scourged the small communities. Sadly two of Kate's sisters died during a diphtheria epidemic.

Miss Wilson's primary education was in Chatsworth, and her High School matriculation was taken in Owen Sound. Later she took secretarial training at Northern Business College, after which she worked briefly in Owen Sound as a journalist. Her older sister had already started a successful career in journalism and young Kate hoped to follow in her footsteps. However when her younger sister came down with tuberculosis, she was forced to leave her job and care for her sister. Over the next few months Kate treated her sister, and her caring manner so impressed the local doctor that he recommended she follow a career in nursing.

In 1910 Kate enrolled in nursing at the Owen Sound Marine Hospital, and for the next three years she trained in her profession. After graduation in 1913 she took up a post as a nurse for the Board of Education, and was under contract there when war was declared in August 1914.

Kate was anxious to enlist but the First Contingent's complement of 101 Nursing Sisters was quickly filled. By 1915 more Sisters were required, and her cousin, who was the Minister of Militia's secretary, gave her a quick heads up. She came to Ottawa and became one of 72 Nursing Sisters to be sent overseas as reinforcements in early 1915. The rest of her story is eloquently told in her memoir.

In late 1916 Kate Wilson came down with influenza. She had endured many hardships and she had served Canada well. In January 1917 Kate went home.

However her story was far from over. She had kept up her romance with the star Wiarton hockey player she had met in France, Robert William Simmie.

Robert Simmie was born in Harriston, Ontario on September 27th, 1889. As an adult he worked in the sawmills and played hockey. In September 1915 he enlisted at Guelph, Ontario, was quickly shipped overseas and by 1916 found himself in the front line, serving as a Lieutenant in the 3rd Battalion, The Toronto Regiment, Canadian Infantry. His first battle came in June 1916 at Mount Sorrel. It was a brutal battle for the Canadians. In less than two weeks they suffered 10,000 killed, wounded and missing. In his first fight Lieutenant Simmie behaved with great coolness and courage. On June 13th, 1916, during the great Canadian counter-attack, he organized the battalion grenade supply and brought forward ammunition under heavy fire. He then held an important trench block for 8 hours. For his bravery he was awarded the Military Cross. During the battle the 3rd Battalion lost 415 men, including 137 killed. Amongst the seriously wounded was Robert Simmie. His wounds would result in the loss of three ribs and part of his hand. While convalescing he went to visit a friend of his sister's, Kate Wilson, and their romance began.

The two continued their relationship in England in late 1916. Shortly after Sister Wilson returned to Canada, Robert followed. In March 1917 she resigned from the Overseas Military Forces of Canada, and on May 7th, 1917, Katharine Wilson married, now Captain, Robert Simmie. He continued service with the Army, acting as a recruiting officer for the British-Canadian mission in Kansas City, Missouri. In April 1918 their first child, Helen, was born there.

After the war they returned to Robert's hometown of Wiarton, where he went into the Car business. Together they had six children, one boy and five girls. At the outbreak of the Second World War, Bob went back to the Army to help with recruiting drives and Kate got involved with the Red Cross.

In 1948 Robert Simmie died suddenly. Kate returned to nursing shortly afterwards, after a refresher course and a heart attack. She was treated at Sunnybrook Hospital where she said "If you got in there you had to bomb yourself out... they wouldn't discharge you until you were absolutely perfect." Kate worked as a nurse in the Public Health Unit in Wiarton until she retired.

Katharine Mildred Wilson-Simmie was described as being a restless personality, a vibrant, energetic person, who was always ready to help. She was involved with the hospitals or with her church, her family and her community. When interviewed in 1977 she was asked about her greatest contribution during World War One. She responded in typical fashion, "I never thought about giving a contribution. I don't think it ever struck me that what I did was a contribution. I was just there to do a job and I did it. And I wouldn't have missed it for anything."

Nursing Sister Kate Wilson died September 5th, 1984. She is buried in Bayview Cemetery, Wiarton, Ontario.